Dominique Achour - Fischer

Real Estate Investment Analysis

For (not complete) idiots

This textbook and its companion website are copyrighted and trademarked

(1992, 2002, 2017)™

ISBN - 13: 978-1979780384

ISBN-10: 1979780382

In this text feminine and masculine pronouns are used randomly.
No gender bias should be implied.

This text is the reproduction of "Investment Property Analysis", FP Media 1999 - Perth, and the translation of "Analyse des Investissements Immobiliers", Montréal, 1992.

Both books are authored by D. Achour-Fischer

The sub-title is an obvious spoof of the famous titles of books ".... for Dummies" and "... for Idiots". No reader should feel offended.

This book is not a full book: it's half a book.

The more stable part of the book is this half: the printed version. This part will be — more or less — permanent. I will not try to keep track of market events or research trends, nor will I try to keep up with bibliographical references (most of the references cited in this version are already hopelessly outdated).

The other half of this book (the web component) will be updated continuously. It will include the Excel calculations required in each chapter, presentation slides for lecturers, databases and pertinent articles.

Access to the Web site:

www.domfischer.wixsite.com/realestate

Cover page illustration

Serigraphy by Lemieu - Québec City - 1978

Une maison dans une rue de Québec.

Contents

Chapter I — Introduction to property analysis	9
1. The property investor's attitude	10
2. Property Assets's characteristics	10
2.1 Location, Location, Location	11
2.2 The asset size	12
2.3 The durability of the asset	13
3. Characteristics of property markets	14
3.1 Market fragmentation	14
3.2 Market opacity	14
3.3 Market viscosity	15
4. Conclusion	15
Chapter II — Financial flows: the basics	19
1. The 'Rozy' building: a first glimpse	20
2. Computing operation flows	21
3. The analytical tree	24
Chapter III — Time is Money, mathematics of finance	27
1. The concept of interest	27
1.1 Simple interest	28
1.2 Compound interest	29
1.3 The frequency of compounding: Nominal Rate, Periodic Rate and Effective Rate	30
2. A voyage through time: the six basic factors	32
2.1 The compounding of a single amount	34
2.2 The discounting of a single amount	35
2.3 The compounding of annuities	36
2.4 Discounting an annuity	36
2.5 The sinking fund annuity	37
2.6 The amortisation factor	38
3. Varia: for further recycling	39
3.1 Perpetual annuities (or perpetuities)	39
3.2 Annuities due	40
3.3 Simple and general annuities	40
4. Present value, net present value and internal rate of return	42
4.1 The present value of two amounts	42
4.2 The internal rate of return	43
4.3 Present value, internal rate and annuities	44
5. Practical conclusion	48
Chapter IV — Property financing	49
1. Paying back a loan	50
1.1 Interest-only loans	50
1.2 Amortised fixed-rate loans	51
1.3 The variable rate amortised loan	55
2. The Australian mortgage (Platypus format ...)	56

3. Applications ... 58
   3.1 The effective cost of a mortgage loan ... 58
4. Practical conclusion ... 61

Chapter V — Elements of property taxation ... 63

1. Taxing operating income ... 65
   1.1 Operation or capital expenditures? ... 65
   1.2 The treatment of financing charges ... 68
   1.3 The treatment of depreciation ... 68
   1.4 The treatment of operating losses ... 72
2. Taxation at disposal ... 72
   2.1 The taxation of capital gains ... 73
   2.2 Recapture on depreciable assets ... 75
   2.3 Rozy meets the tax person ... 76

Chapter VI — Investment return measurement ... 79

1. Static indicators ... 79
   1.1 Static indicators of performance ... 80
   1.2 Operating and financial indicators of performance ... 85
2. Dynamic return measurements ... 88
   2.1 The general equity model ... 88
   2.2 The Net Present Value ... 90
   2.3 The Internal Rate of Return ... 90
   2.4 The Maximum Bidding Price (MBP) ... 91
3. The full tool box ... 92
   3.1 Static instruments ... 92
   3.2 Dynamic indicators and instruments ... 92
4. Practical conclusion ... 93

Chapter VII — How much to pay? (or to sell ...) ... 95

1. Simplified discounted cash flows ... 96
2. The Full Monty ... 100
3. Calculating equity flows ... 101
   3.1 The tax route ... 101
   3.2 The cash flow route ... 102
   3.3 Allocating the operating flows ... 103
4. Calculating disposal cash flows ... 104
   4.1 Analysing disposition via the tax route ... 104
   4.2 Disposition via the cash flow route ... 105
   4.3 The allocation of disposal flows ... 106
5. Valuing the investment ... 107
6. Conclusion ... 109

Chapter VIII — Property risk analysis ... 111

1. Risk taking: defined and dissected ... 111
   1.1 Risk and uncertainty ... 111
   1.2 Dissecting risk ... 112
   1.3 Exposure to business and financial risk ... 113
2. Risk measurement ... 116
   2.1 Probability distributions ... 116
   2.2 Measuring dispersion and assessing risk ... 119

3. Single project risk analysis		125
3.1 Tuning for risk		125
4. Running the risk		129
4.1 Sensitivity analysis		130
4.2 Monte Carlo simulation (probabilistic simulations)		133
5. Conclusion		135

Appendix VI.1   137

Performance measurements: bells and whistles ...   137

Appendix VI.2   143

Return and financial leverage   143

Appendix VI.3   149

The Napkin and Yoyo techniques   149

Appendix VII.1   153

The negative about negative gearing   153

Appendix VIII.1   155

A Further drawback of the Internal Rate of Return   155

Chapter I

Introduction to property analysis

Where we deal with the main characteristics of property assets and where we consider how these characteristics affect the investment behaviour and analytical tools of investors.

Neither bricks nor architectural masterpiece, in this textbook, a property is simply treated as a stream of cash flows. To the promoter, the architect or the urban tourist, this may seem to be a crass view of the world, however it is the only perspective allowing the investor, the analyst and the property valuer to judge the worth of a property. Figure 1.1 presents a graphic representation of an investment property:

Figure I.1

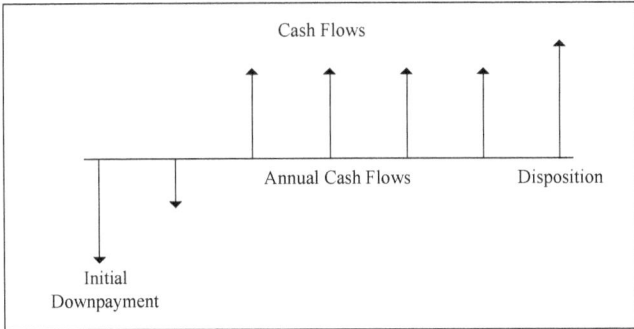

This graph summarizes all the financial traits of a property investment: the initial cash down investment, the after-tax and after-debt cash flows and the net proceeds most likely to be realised at disposal time.

This approach allows us to cut through all the circumstantial features that may clog the analysis and, even more importantly, it enables us to apply techniques which have been adopted in the traditional field of corporate finance over the last thirty years.

However, this analogy with corporate finance should not be pushed too far because property assets and markets differ sufficiently from other financial instrument markets (bonds, common stocks, collectable) to warrant our special attention.

These differences stem from three sets of factors:

— factors related to the investor's financial 'philosophy';
— factors related to the asset's peculiarities;
— finally, factors related to specific traits of the property markets.

1. The property investor's attitude

The typical property investor may be more concerned with the resale potential of an asset than with its annual 'dividends'. For many (but not all) investors, the primary concern is whether the property will ultimately increase its resale value even if this implies the temporary acceptance of annual negative cash flows. This philosophy is changing in countries where inflation is abating and, among the largest property players, 'institutional' investors are increasingly interested in the regularity and security of annual cash flows.

When he does care about annual cash flows, the property investor must consider after-debt and after-tax cash flows (net of debt and net of tax flows). Thus financing and taxation features become an integral part of any property investment decision. In particular, the effect of financial leverage is one of the most attractive (and dangerous) features of this type of investment since the financing element is such a massive component of any property investment.

In view of the highly leveraged situation of most investments, the property investor is (or should be) quite attentive to the high level of risk involved in this form of venture. Because of this risk exposure she demands a much higher return on her equity capital than she would expect from a blue-chip-no-insomnia type of investment.

This relationship between the level of risk borne by the investor and the expected return is one of the *leitmotiv* of general financial theory and we will use it later to choose the proper return and discount rates required to perform a project analysis.

2. Property Assets's characteristics

Property assets (land, housing units, residential rental properties, shopping centres, etc.) have specific features which must be emphasized if we want to understand the behaviour of the markets on which these assets are produced, consumed and transacted. These features are (1) the importance of location, (2) the relatively large size of the asset and (3) the durability of the asset.

2.1 Location, Location, Location

By its very nature, a property asset is immobile (in French, the word for property is *immobilier*. Even better, in Mexican spanish property assets are described as 'rooted goods': *Bienes raices)*. Not only can you not move a house, a shopping centre or a factory, but moreover, neither can you modify its physical surroundings. A property is entirely dependent on its environment and this dependence makes comparisons among similar units quite difficult. For example, it makes little sense to compare two shopping centres if we have no information on their respective transportation network. To take an extreme case, we could even imagine that contiguous properties, being otherwise indistinguishable, may command very different prices. Compare for example the values of two similar neighbouring houses with one facing the sea and the other (for some goofy reason) facing the municipal dump.

In economist's jargon we say that property assets are heterogeneous (each differing from the others) and that they are subject to market externalities: their use and value is influenced by 'external' factors.

— Such externalities can be positive: a new subway station does wonders to the value of nearby commercial properties; a busy highway boosts the value of a shopping centre and the construction of classy mansions pushes the prices of neighbouring units.

— Externalities can also be negative: the proximity of a foul smelling factory, a noisy thoroughfare or a disreputable commercial activity will depress the value of properties in the area.

— And to make things a bit more interesting, some factors may have positive effects on certain properties and negative ones on others. For instance, a large parking lot is good for the shopping centre but not so good for residential neighbours.

The spatial specificity of property assets must also be seen in a wider context. Every area, city, region and country has its own market traits and their price structures are not comparable. Clearly, property prices in Perth are different from those in Kalamunda, but they differ even more widely from prices in Singapore, Oulan-Bator, Bujumbura and Hong Kong.

The worn out property *cliché* about the three main determinants of value (location, location and location) could find renewed meaning if we broaden the conception of the word 'location'.

Spatial location (or geographic location) has just been discussed. The physical location of a property explains most of its value and its marketability. In some way, each unit enjoys a spatial monopoly. If the location is favourable, this monopoly will be exploited by the owner who will charge higher rents and so assure himself of a higher resale value.

The temporal location of a project would be defined more simply as its timing. Good timing (when demand is high and supply is low) confers a temporary monopoly on the project and again, this will lead to higher rents and higher values. Of course this advantageous 'location' may be short-lived, but the lead time enjoyed by a well timed project may be enough to improve the investment's long term return.

The *niche* location is a less familiar concept imported from marketing lingo: it indicates the 'location' (the positioning) of a product within the range of existing products. A favourable *niche*, once more, confers a form of monopoly and with it, higher returns until product imitators catch up with the innovation. Examples of such *niche* location leaders include the shopping centres of the sixties, suburban developments of the seventies or golf based projects of the nineties. This niche markets of this decade may be a mixed bag of downtown cappuccino flavoured apartments and any form of beachified residential development (in coastal Australia at least). And, if anyone is looking for the next *niche*, they should start investigated all forms of geronto-housing formulas.

This overhaul of the 'location-location-location' *cliché* should also stress the relativity of favourable or unfavourable locations. Whether dealing with spatial, temporal or *niche* location, we should remember that time and events can easily alter the meaning of the *cliché*. The history of property is a very long story of the rise and fall of entire cities, villages and communities. Even within a very short time frame, it may be wise to recall, the decay and *renaissance* of Manhattan (an effect of spatial location), the roller coaster swings of condo prices in Florida (an effect of temporal location) and the vagaries of time sharing projects (an effect of *niche* location).

2.2 The asset size

Property assets are 'big' assets that weigh heavily in the budget and portfolio of most households and firms. Housing expenses typically devour the lion's share of the household consumption budget and, in Australia, they account for over 70% of a households' net assets. Firms (especially manufacturing firms) must also allocate a major chunk of their resources to property capital in the form of factories, warehouses, offices and land.

For the property supplier (builder, developer or manager), the size and lumpiness of the product explains why it is quite difficult for him to adjust quickly to demand. It is impossible to produce one square metre, one apartment or one office at a time. The producer must attain a certain threshold in demand before he can start building. When he builds on anticipated demand ("spec building"), he risks missing his exact target and his project may be under or oversized.

Furthermore, because property projects are 'big' ventures, they are also quite lengthy ones. It takes many months or years to plan, build and market a product and again, for this reason, it is harder to satisfy demand on a timely fashion.

This consequence of the assets' size is one of the major causes behind the hit and miss nature of the business and may explains its chronic instability.

For consumers, the size constraint explains the rigidity of housing decisions: it is always costly and sometimes impossible to enlarge or reduce the size of the dwellings according to the household's needs. For example, the birth of children often necessitate a move. Like snails, households must often change their abode to meet evolving needs: from the newlyweds' studio, to the family bungalow and the 'wellderly' condos.

The same 'size rigidity' applies to firms and businesses: they must either move or adjust their space utilization and these adjustments are always costly and disruptive.

Property is also a sizable asset in the financial sense of the word and thus, it almost always involves some form of long term financing. Furthermore, because of its large size, a property investment is not a good financial instrument for diversification: unless you have a large basket, your property egg is likely to be your only egg.

2.3 The durability of the asset

Buildings are not only 'big', they are also durable. This, combined with the large size of the asset, contributes to the lack of flexibility in the production and consumption of real properties.

Property is made up of a permanent land component and a 'temporary' building component whose life may span fifty years; well beyond if well tended and restored. Thus, for our purposes, property properties can be treated as physically eternal assets.

Physical durability aside, what really matters is the economic longevity of an investment: its capacity to produce an adequate stream of income. A property reaches the end of its economic life when the returns fall below the returns which could be obtained from similar alternative investments; and, in most cases, this economic life is shorter than the physical life. Indeed, the economic usefulness of a property can be very short in some specific commercial utilisations (restaurants, hotels, speciality boutiques, etc.). At the end of a property's productive life the use should be changed; failing this, the building could be demolished and rebuilt in a different configuration. At any time the objective of the investor is to obtain the highest and best use of his property and this optimal use may involve the transformation or the demolition of the property. For example, well preserved office buildings are routinely torn down; garages can be converted into mini shopping centres; motels into residences for the aged and, of course, the 'in thing' nowadays, decrepit warehouses and factories can be turned into luxurious condominiums.

So far property assets have been described as:

— heterogeneous: no two properties being exactly the same. They differ at least in their physical location, possibly more so by their nature and functions (dwellings, factories, shopping centres, office buildings, amusement parks, hotels, cemeteries);

— indivisible: being big and durable, property properties cannot readily be delivered or consumed in small increments. This indivisibility is responsible for most of the adjustment difficulties in this industry and explains why property investments are not the ideal platform on which to build a diversified portfolio for most households.

Thus, property assets lack two of the attributes which are normally used to define the functioning of a competitive market. Let us now briefly check if the other conditions[1] are fulfilled.

3. Characteristics of property markets

3.1 Market fragmentation

One should not even use the word property 'market' in its singular form since we are dealing with a complex hierarchy of sub-markets and sub-sub-markets. The market should at least be divided amongst the broad categories of residential, commercial and industrial markets (and all their sub-markets). Then each country, each city and even each area within a city forms another set of sub-markets. Each market has its own price structure and follows different demand trends. Of course, the numerous sub-markets of a national or regional market are strongly interrelated, but major timing and pricing differences should always be taken into account by investors and analysts.

3.2 Market opacity

Property transactions do not have the same visibility as share market transactions. Property transactions are less frequent, less visible and they are often conducted behind closed doors. Furthermore, since these operations occur in a very fragmented market, even the visible part of the market is not enough to 'read' the different sub-markets accurately.

In fact, market opacity (*i.e.,* its lack of transparency) is the *raison d'être* of property professionals. Brokers, valuers and lawyers thrive on the fact that consumers and investors do not have direct access to information on prices and quantities. Not surprisingly, a comprehensive information system and data bank on real properties has yet to be organized. Such a system, similar to a

---

1. A purely competitive market is usually defined by the perfect divisibility and homogeneity of the product, and its unicity (a single market), its atomicity (a large number of small producers and consumers), its transparency (the immediate availability of information on prices and quantities) and its fluidity (the possibility to enter and exit the market at no cost). By contrast, the property market can be characterized by its fragmentation (vs. unicity), its opacity (vs. transparency) and its viscosity (vs. fluidity).

stock exchange institution, may conflict with the best interests of these professionals and cost them their enviable hold on information.

3.3 Market viscosity

It is relatively easy to enter (and to exit) the property market for an investor or developer, but this entry-exit is not without cost. Not only are information costs high due to market opacity, but so are transactions costs. Legal, professional and brokerage fees can easily skim 8% to 10% off a typical transaction compared to less than 1% percent brokerage fee levied on share deals. High transaction costs is another reason why it is difficult to diversify and fine tune a portfolio of property assets.

4. Conclusion

The market for real properties is fragmented, opaque and viscous and cannot support well the usual hypothesis of a pure competitive market. Nevertheless, we will have to assume that these market imperfections are not severe enough for us to reject the whole set of instruments and theories normally applied to competitive markets.

Consequently, most of our discussions will adhere to the paradigm of standard economic and financial analysis. To be more specific, we will rely on models based on the premise that property markets are efficient. In our limited use of the word, the efficiency hypothesis implies that property prices fully incorporate all perceived advantages and information concerning the property and the market. In simpler terms, the concept of market efficiency means at least two things:

- Investors are not stupid: the price they pay reflects market conditions and market values.
- Property assets are not money machines and cannot expected to be miraculous investments.

Table I.1 Pros and cons of property assets

Pros	Yes, but ...
High returns	Commensurate with higher risk.
High level of gearing	Higher leverage implies a higher level of risk.
Inflation protection	It depends where the property is located (countries, regions or even part of town).
Tax advantages	Any tax advantage is likely to be capitalised in the asset's value.
Tangibility	Yes, however tangible also means immobile.
Potential for capital gain	The expectation of future capital gains is also incorporated in the price paid now.
Residential properties can be lived in	But this does not mean that the owner does not bear rental charges. In fact the implicit (inputted) rent level could be higher than normal market rents.
Instrument of diversification	Not at all ... on the contrary. There is a growing tendency to over-weight property assets. Particularly dangerous when property assets are combined with human assets (jobs) in the same location.
Durability	... so poor investments can haunt you for a very long time. Combined with property assets big size, durability reduces the possibilities of diversification
Benefits from positive externalities	Suffers from negative externalities.
	Illiquidity and high transaction costs.
	Property markets are fragmented and thus make comparison more difficult.
	Property markets are opaque and thus investors cannot easily determine market prices.

Table I.2 Property assets are increasingly 'paperised'

The direct or indirect securitisation of property assets can take many forms.
Listed property trusts (LPT)
Unlisted property trusts
Property syndicates
Property trust bonds
Mortgage backed securities (MBS)
Commercial mortgage backed securities (CMBS)
Multi-options pre-sale securitisation (MOPS)

Check your IPA Website for updated information on the major forms of paperised property investments.

Chapter II

Financial flows: the basics

A very short chapter where we define the jargon and learn to draw a tree. Where we introduce a building named 'Rozy' which will serve as the main example for following chapters.

In the first chapter we reduced a building to a mere flow of expenses and incomes spread over its holding period. It was a convenient simplification, but now we have to define and illustrate the concepts of 'incomes' and 'expenses' more precisely. This exercise in definition is particularly important since property jargon differs slightly but significantly from that used in corporate finance and accounting. Unfortunately, we also have some confusion between expressions used in Australia (and other UK-sphere countries) and in the US (and US-sphere countries). In this text, we will try to clarify the concepts in order to avoid some of the major sources of misunderstanding.

The analyst's objective is to forecast a property's main financial characteristics. What matters to her is the amount of cash left in her pocket at the end of each year having satisfied her banker (mortgage payments) and the tax collector (taxes owing on the property's income). This estimation of cash residuals is performed in the spirit of the accrual method of accounting: expenses and revenues are accounted for when they are due, irrespective of when they are in fact paid or received. The valuer and the analyst are mainly concerned with the potential and normal productive capacity of a property — they should avoid getting bogged down with the accounting details.

It is important to realise that property analysis is essentially an exercise in midterm forecasting of incomes, expenses and resale values. Such a predictive treatment cannot be overly accurate. On the contrary, excessive accuracy only points to a poor understanding of the valuation procedure.

Let us return to the cash flow pattern described in the figure 1.1 and, this time, carefully distinguish between: 1) the property's operating period, and 2) the disposal of the property.

1. The 'Rozy' building: a first glimpse

To illustrate our discussions, we now introduce a textbook type case: a very simple and nicely rounded prototype residential building whose particulars appear in Table II.1. The same example will be used in future chapters with a few added bells and whistles.

Table II.1 The Rozy Building

Total value on purchase date	100,000$[1]
Value of the building	70,000$
Value of the land	20,000$
Value of plant and fixtures	10,000$
Debt to Value Ratio	80%
Mortgage loan	80,000$
Nominal rate	6%
Amortisation	15 years
Marginal rate of taxation (individual investor)	48%
After-tax cash flows discount rate	10%
Reversion value[2] (10 times net operating income in year 6)	121,008$
Transaction costs	4%
Initial potential gross income	15,000$
Growing at a yearly rate of	5%
Initial operating expenses (% of potential gross income)	35%
Growing at a yearly rate of	3%
Vacancy rate	5%

Though we cannot as yet explain all the calculations in detail, we can at least follow the basic computational steps shown in Figure II.1.

---

1. The $ after the number **is** intentional. The justification of this hybrid notation was offered at the beginning of the book.

2. **Reversion** value = resale value = disposition value ('disposal' is the preferred expression in Australia). The word 'Reversion' is used in the UK-sphere literature to describe the adjustment (usually upward) of the rent level at the end of a leasing period. It may not imply that the property is disposed of. In this text, we will not use this UK meaning and, generally, we will try to stick to the more universal US-sphere terms and conventions.

Figure II.1

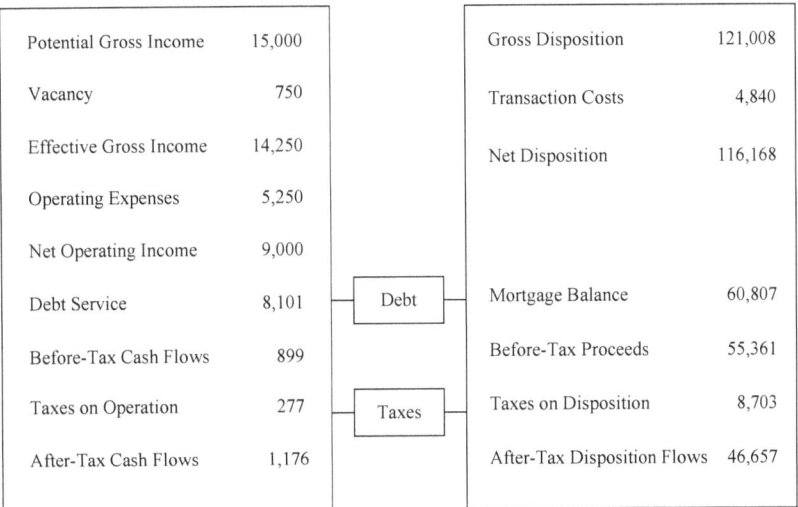

2. Computing operation flows

PGI

The **Potential Gross Income** refers to the highest revenue obtainable from a given property. In residential buildings this includes apartment rentals, parking rentals, laundry room revenues and, eventually, commercial rents from stores or offices occupying part of the building.

For valuation purposes, the gross income information provided by the owner must be verified and compared with the operating performances of similar properties located in the same general area. Should the subject property offer a different range of services to its tenants (furnishing, doorman, security, swimming pool, etc.), the valuer must also carry out adjustments to qualify the comparison.

In a shopping centre, the potential gross income will, in addition to the basic space rental, include participation revenues computed on each store's activity. It will also include the share of expenses that are borne by the tenants.

In office buildings, the potential gross income includes all the lease revenues and ancillary incomes. The tenants' share of expenses may also be added.

> **VAC**

Rarely can the owner achieve the full potential rent on a property. He must account for the likely **vacancy** losses and bad debts. Even in a fully occupied building one must anticipate frictional vacancies and some rental income will be lost due to tenant mobility. Some days are inevitably lost to refurbishing and to tenant change over.

In addition to vacancies, a certain percentage of bad debts must be deducted from the potential gross income. This deduction should not be treated as an accounting reserve but as a likely loss of income.

In some cases it may also be useful to single out sources of vacancy. For example, different rates could be applied to the housing units, the parking lots or the commercial areas in a multi function type of property.

> **EGI**

Having deducted the anticipated losses for vacancies and bad debts, we are left with the **Effective Gross Income** which gives a sharper picture of the building's operation. The performance indicators computed on gross income (see Chapter VI) should be calculated on effective income, not on potential income. Unfortunately, the proper adjustments are not always submitted to the unsuspecting investor: the numbers always look slightly better when a building is offered for sale.

> **OE**

Operating Expenses (or outgoings) are numerous and diverse; they include repairs and maintenance expenditures, utilities, local taxes and rates, insurance premiums, advertising, snow removal, pest control, wages and employee benefits, management and consultant fees, etc. For a residential property, these disbursements can amount to 30% to 50% of potential gross income.

As we shall see in Chapter V, for the purposes of tax calculation, operation expenditures must not include capital expenditures or professional and legal fees which are incurred during the construction or acquisition phases. Only outlays expended to maintain the property in a good state of repair are deductable during the years of operation. Capital expenditures, which contribute to the appreciation of the property, are either amortised separately or incorporated into the adjusted cost basis of the building and fixtures. Thus, for tax reasons, we may have to adjust our cash flow computations in order to sort out capital expenditures and operating expenditures.

When certain expenditures are borne by the tenants (lessees), as is usually the case for commercial properties, only the owner's (lessor) share of expenses must be considered. Rental conditions in shopping centres and office buildings can be quite diverse and complex. They run the full gamut from the pure 'gross rent' where all costs are borne by the owner to the 'net-net-net' (triple net lease or fully net lease) where the tenants are responsible for most of the charges (equipment, maintenance, energy, insurance and taxes). The general trend is for owners to try and obtain the 'netest' possible leases so that most of the risks are born by the tenants.

However, the recent Western Australian new Commercial Tenancy Agreements Act may be pushing for the generalisation of Gross leasing. A gross rent is a flat all inclusive amount; it covers the base rent and variable outgoings that were previously charged back to the tenants. This opposite trend can be explained by the legal and administrative exigencies of the Act that require a much greater transparency in the allocation of operating charges to the tenants.

When some outgoings are assumed by the lessor (taxes, energy, etc.), escalation clauses are frequently included. Such escalation conditions allow the owner to index the rent to the variation of expenditures and assures him a protection against inflation. Once all operating expenses are subtracted, we are left with the net operating income.

| NOI |

The **Net Operating Income** is the most general indication of a property's income potential before debt and taxes. At this neutral level, one does not have to consider the financing and taxation conditions of the investor which explains why this stage of analysis is the most appropriate for appraisal purposes. Most of the so-called income techniques used in valuation rely on this NOI stage as the basis for establishing value. Australian and British texts sometimes define this net income as a 'Cash Flow'. This practice is quite confusing and should not be encouraged since, as we shall see shortly, the term 'cash flow' has a specific and different meaning.

| BTCF |

The term 'cash', as in the normal English usage, applies to 'what's left in your pocket', thus the first level of cash flow, the **Before-Tax Cash Flow,** is obtained by the deduction of the annual mortgage payments (interest and principal). In financial parlance, we would say that we split the Net Operating Income between the titleholder and the equity investor. The titleholder receives the fruits of the mortgage and the equity owner receives the leftovers that still have to be shared with the Tax Office.

| DEP |

The **depreciation** should reflect the potential annual loss in value of the building and equipment. Much more will be said about this matter in the chapter dealing with taxation (Chapter V).

| TAXES |

After subtracting interest charges and the annual depreciation and building allowance, we reach the Taxable Income to which we apply the investor's marginal tax rate and find the annual operating tax load on the property.

> ATCF

When, finally, taxes are deducted from the before-tax cash flow we obtain the **After-Tax Cash Flow**.

In property analysis, our prime concern rests with this last stage of our analysis since this residual cash is what is left in the investor's pocket when he has satisfied the titleholder and the tax collector ('Cash after the Bank and after the Queen...'). Later in Chapter VI, we will perform our present value analysis on the basis of this 'after-debt, after-tax' cash flow since it the best indicator of a property's true investment value.

3. The analytical tree

The analytical tree in Figure II.2 will help us illustrate the entire process:

1. One must start at the top of the tree and then descend the right side of the figure in order to compute operating taxes. The interest on the various debts and depreciations are deducted and the investor's marginal tax rate is applied to the resulting taxable income.

2. Then, on the left side, the true cash outflows are deducted (the full debt service and operating taxes) to reach the 'net net' cash flows (after-tax cash flows: ATCF).

The layout standards of a property's operating flows are not very strict and, even for public companies, the depth of detail provided to the investor can vary widely between firms, between countries and between types of properties. The IPAV companion spreadsheet examples present some real cases (Perth, Singapore) in order to illustrate some typical outgoing categories. These spreadsheets should be constantly updated by the readers in order to provide a regular source of benchmarking for various types and properties[1].

For the time being, the reader should simply observe the different expense and revenue items and get a feel for their order of magnitude. Pending a long detour through chapters IV to VI, we will then be able perform the full investment analysis required to determine the negotiation value of such properties.

Another detour may also be required for the reader who would benefit from a refresher in financial mathematics. In fact, most readers — even the calculator virtuoso — should go through Chapter III to get acquainted with our notation; otherwise, the rest of this textbook will seem quite quaint indeed.

---

1. See the IPA website for annually updated information on Australian properties outgoings.

Figure II.2

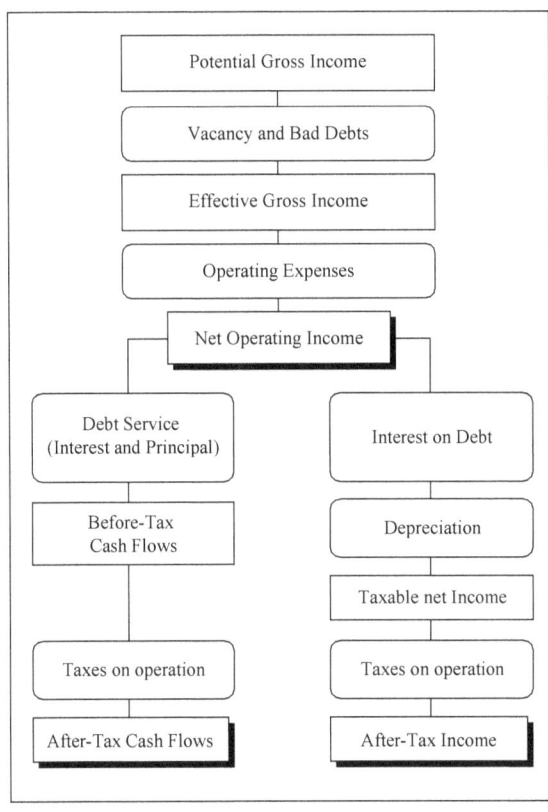

Chapter III

Time is Money, *mathematics of finance*

Where we deal with the basic tools which will enable us to compare amounts or flows of dollars paid or received at different points in time. Where we introduce a coherent notation system to follow us for the remainder of this textbook and where we introduce two of the most important indicators of an investment's value.

Time is money, more than a simple time management proverb, this adage lies at the very core of financial analysis — all the more so in property decisions. Time turns into money when interest accumulates on a sum invested or borrowed. Time also modifies the value of money; any amount to be paid or received in the future is not worth as much as the same amount to be received or paid now.

The elementary concepts of financial mathematics presented in this chapter form the indispensable backbone of this and most other similar courses in real estate or investment analysis. It should be stressed that the rest of this textbook will be indecipherable to the reader who does not master this material and the notation chosen herein.[1]

1. The concept of interest

Interest is the price of money on a deposit or a loan. This price is paid for the use of money during a certain period and it should compensate the lender for the uncertainty of the future value of the amount deposited (inflation being the major reason for this), the risk of not recovering the full amount invested and the sacrifice of deferring the consumption of goods and services. We shall note:

i   the interest rate

PV   the principal or capital: the amount deposited or borrowed today

FV   the total amount to pay back or to receive in the future after n periods

FV - PV = I   the total amount of interest paid or received over the n periods

---

1. This notation was introduced by G. Grant and G. Irenson, *Principles of Engineering Economics*, 1939; and is now the standard notation in the discipline of engineering economics.

1.1 Simple interest

Simple interest accumulates periodically, is calculated on the initial principal amount and paid as a lump sum at the end of n periods.[1]

FV = PV (1 + n × i)

I = PV × i × n

Example: 1 000$ is deposited for 3 years at the simple interest rate of 5%.

PV = 1,000$

i = 5%

n = 3

Let's compute:

I = 1,000$ × 0.05 × 3

= 150$

FV = 1 000$ (1 + 0.05 × 3)

= 1,150$

Simple interest applications are not very common with the exception of some cases of interim and construction financing. In these cases, the interest is usually stated on an annual basis but computed on the number of days that have elapsed in the year (360, 365 or 366 days year according to local custom).

We could write:

I = PV × i × n/365

Example: 100,000$ is borrowed on January 1, 1999 and is due back July 31, 2000. The simple interest rate is 14% per annum.

The interest payment is given by:

I = PV × i × n/365

And the data provided:

PV = 100,000$

i = 14%

= 14/100

= 0.14

n = number of days

= 212 - 1 = 211

---

1. In this text, the symbols "×", "." or conventional factoring such as: P(1 + n.i) are used interchangeably to denote multiplication.

The full repayment is therefore:

FV = PV + I
   = 100,000.00$ + 8,093.15$
   = 108,093.15$

All calculations are presented in the accompanying IPAV spreadsheet. The examples are offered to help you check your calculator practices and, of course, to improve your Excel skills.

1.2 Compound interest

Compound interest is calculated on each periodic balance to which the previous interest has been added. In the previous example, the compounding of interest would give:

For the first year:

P_1 = 1,000$
I_1 = 1,000$ ¥ 0.05
    = 50$

For the second year:

P_2 = $P_1 + I_1$
    = 1,050$
I_2 = P_2 ¥ i
    = 1,050$ ¥ 0.05
    = 52.50$

For the third year:

P_3 = $P_2 + I_2$
    = 1,102.50$
I_3 = P_3 ¥ i
    = 1,102.50$ ¥ 0.05
    = 55.125$

Thus the total amount will be:

FV = 1,000$ + (50.00$ + 52.50$ + 55.125$)
   = 1,157.62$

And the process could be described graphically:

FV = 1,000 ¥ (1+0.05) ¥ (1+0.05) ¥ (1+0.05)

First compounding to get 1,050$ by the end of the first year

Second compounding to get 1,102.50$ by the end of the second year

Third compounding to get 1,157.62$ by the end of the third year

The general formulation of the compounding process would thus be written:

1st : $PV + PV \times i = P_1$

2nd : $P_1 + P_1 \times i = PV(1+i)(1+i) = P_2$

3rd : $P_2 + P_2 \times i = PV(1+i)^2(1+i) = PV(1+i)^3 = P_3$

n^e : $P_{n-1} + P_{n-1} \times i = PV(1+i)^{n-1}(1+i) = PV(1+i)^n = P_n$

And presented in a more compact fashion:

$FV = PV(1+i)^n$

A numerical example of compounding is found in Table III.1.

Table III.1 The compounding process

Years	Principal	Interest	Accumulated amount
n	PV	I	FV_n
0	1,000$		
1		50.00$	1,050.00$
2		52.50$	1,102.50$
3		55.12$	1,157.62$

Compounding computations can be performed in four different ways:

— Using pre-calculated financial tables where the $(1+i)^n$ factor is given for different values of i and n. You only have to find the proper factor and multiply it by PV, the amount deposited or borrowed now;

— Using a rudimentary calculator and repetitively performing the multiplication by $(1+i)$;

— Using the exponential functions on the calculator to raise $(1+i)$ to the nth power and multiply the result by PV;

— Finally, and preferably, one should use the financial functions found on most calculators.

1.3 The frequency of compounding: Nominal Rate, Periodic Rate and Effective Rate

So far we have assumed that interest is added once a year to the yearly balance. We would thus define this as annual compounding or more generally as an annual conversion. However, it is quite common to have different conversion periods: a shorter conversion period for a faster accumulation of interest or, though seldom, a longer conversion over more than a year.

For example, we could use a half-year compounding cycle. The effects of such a semiannual compounding are described on the accumulation of an initial amount of 5,000$ over 35 years:

PV = 5,000$

i   = 10% per year (the annual rate)

n   = 35 years

The periodic interest rate is now 5% (per semester) and n is 70 semesters.

$$FV = 5{,}000\$ \times (1+0.05)^{70}$$
$$= 5{,}000\$ \times 30.426425$$
$$= 152{,}132.12\$$$

Now let's vary the conversion periods to construct Table III.2 using the required notation:

c	=	number of conversion periods per year
i	=	the nominal (annual) rate
p_c	=	the rate per conversion period
n	=	the total number of conversion periods

Table III.2 Capitalisation of an amount using different conversions

Conversion period	Nominal rate	Periodic rate	Periods	Factor	FV	Effective rate
c	i	p_c				
1 year	0.10	0.10	35	28.102	140,512.18	0.10
1 semester	0.10	0.05	70	30.426	152,132.12	0.1025
1 quarter	0.10	0.025	140	31.720	158,602.91	0.1038
1 month	0.10	0.00833	420	32.638	163,193.24	0.1047

We must insist on the proper definition of the different rates: the nominal rate, the periodic rate and the effective rate. The nominal rate is equal to the periodic rate multiplied by the number of conversions periods in a year.

We write:

$$i_c = \text{the nominal rate}$$
$$i_c = p_c \times c$$

Where p_c is the periodic interest rate (per conversion period) and c is the number of conversion periods in a year (c should not be confused with n which represents the total number of conversion periods over the whole term of the operation). Thus, in the previous example, the nominal rate was 10% and the periodic rate p_c was 5%. We write:

$$i_c = p_c \times c$$
$$i_2 = 5\% \times 2$$

A nominal rate of 18% with semiannual compounding means a periodic rate of 9%:

$$i_2 = p_c \times c$$
$$i_2 = 18\%$$
$$18\% = p_c \times 2$$
$$p_c = 18\%/2$$
$$p_c = 9\%$$

A nominal rate of 20% and a periodic rate of 5% implies quarterly compounding (there being 4 quarters in a year):

$i_c = p_c \times c$
$i_c = 20\%$
$20\% = 5\% \times c$
$c = 20\%/5\%$
$c = 4$

The effective annual rate i_e is the annual equivalent of a given periodic rate. We shall write, for a one year period, the compounding factor:

$(1 + i_e) = (1 + p_c)^c$
$i_e = (1 + p_c)^c - 1$

Thus in the previous example, the effective rate for a nominal rate of 10% and semiannual conversion is:

$i_e = (1 + p_c)^c - 1$
$ = (1 + 0.10/2)^2 - 1$
$i_e = 10.25\%$

With a quarterly conversion (c = 4) the effective rate is:

$i_e = (1 + p_c)^c - 1$
$ = (1 + 0.10/4)^4 - 1$
$i_e = 10.38\%$

And for monthly conversions (c = 12) the effective rate is:

$i_e = (1 + p_c)^c - 1$
$ = (1 + 0.10/12)^{12} - 1$
$i_e = 10.47\%$

We must insist, for the last time, on the semantics: a nominal rate is an annual rate (by definition) and an effective rate is also an annual rate. The expression "annual rate" is not quite explicit enough to indicate whether we are dealing with a nominal or an effective rate: it is imperative to distinguish these "annual" rates.

2. A voyage through time: the six basic factors

Up to now we have observed how an amount borrowed or deposited today will earn interest and grow into a larger amount to be paid or redeemed in the future. We called this the compounding process *i.e.*, the passage from the present into the future. Now we could move backward and transform a future amount (to be received or to be paid) into its equivalent present value: this reverse time trip will be defined as the discounting process. Furthermore, we shall see that not only single amounts (present or future), but also regular flows of payments can also be compounded or discounted.

Six basic time translations can be performed on money: the discounting and compounding of single amounts, the discounting or compounding of flows of payments, and the accumulation or depletion of amounts through a regular flow of payments or withdrawals. Each of these will be treated in the following paragraphs:

2.1 The compounding of a single amount

2.2 The discounting of a single amount

2.3 The compounding of a regular flow of payments

2.4 The discounting of a regular flow of payments

2.5 The compounding of a regular flow to build up a future amount

2.6 The discounting of a present amount into a flow of payments

La Barata[1]

The simplest and cheapest of all calculators will be used as the model of all financial instruments based on the 5 financial functions. For the sake of commercial neutrality[2] this paper model will represent the standard procedure applicable to all computations This procedure is perfectly analogical with the notation of our symbolic formulas where 3 variables are known and we compute the missing fourth.[3]

(**Unknown variable**/Known variable , i% , n periods)

Thus, in the case of the computing of a single amount, the process is illustrated below with La Barata:

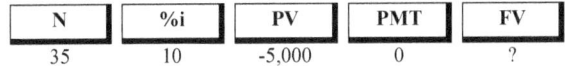

N	%i	PV	PMT	FV
35	10	-5,000	0	?

The unknown variable FV is computed to be 140,512.18$.

It should be noted that the PV value is entered as a negative number (disbursement) to obtain a positive FV value (to be received) and conversely: a +PV would result in a -FV. This sign convention is typical of most calculators but may be different on the simplest models of Texas Instrument tools.

Notations

In symbolic formulas (unit factors)	In dollars amounts and keys on calculators	
F	FV	Future Value
P	PV	Present Value
A	PMT	Annuity (Payment)

1. *Barata* = 'cheap' in Spanish. Forgive the pun...
2. The Spanish version of this textbook uses the HP-12C, the French (France) version uses the BA.54 and the French (Canada) version uses the more recent HP-19B.
3. Later we will also deal with situations where the firsts 4 variables are known and we compute the missing fifth variable.

2.1 The compounding of a single amount

The future value FV of a present amount PV compounded at the rate i over n periods is written:

FV = PV $(1 + i)^n$

Graphically the compounding of a single amount looks like this:

Figure III.1

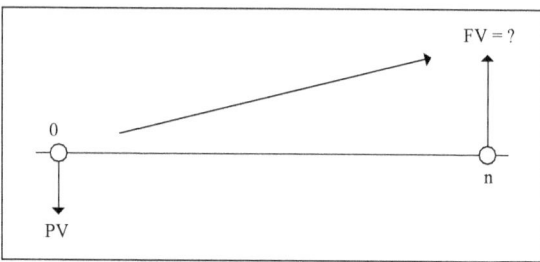

Symbolically the compounding factor $(1 +i)^n$ could be written:

(FV/PV , i , n) = $(1 + i)^n$

Or, when using factors of 1$ we will be noting, as in the initial Irenson and Grant notation:

F = Future, instead of FV

P = Present, instead of PV

Thus, the symbolic notation will be:

(**F**/P , i , n)

(**Unknown value**/Known value , i% , n periods)

This notation reads: what is the future value (**F?**, unknown) of a current 1$ (P, known) compounded at i% over n periods?

The notation FV and PV will be reserved for $ amounts.

Example: what is the future value of 5,000$ deposited today at 10% for 35 years?

FV = PV ¥ (F/P , i , n)
   = 5,000$ ¥ (F/P , 10% , 35 years)
   = 5,000$ ¥ 28.1024

FV = 140,512.18$

On a financial calculator, we simply enter 5,000 for PV, 10 for i and 35 for n; the resulting FV is the future value we are looking for. Let's stress the analogy between our symbolic notation and the way we enter the information into the calculator:

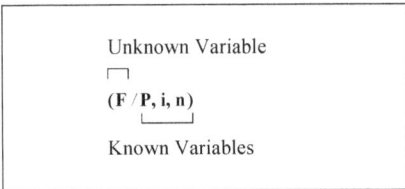

2.2 The discounting of a single amount

Suppose we turn the question around and want to find the present value of a sum to be paid or received at some time in the future. Predictably, the formula is the mathematical inverse of the preceding factor:

$$PV = FV \times \frac{1}{(1+i)^n} = FV(1+i)^{-n}$$

Symbolically:

$(P/F, i, n) = (1 + i)^{-n}$

And reads: what is the present value (P?) of a future 1$ (F) to pay or receive in n years if the discount rate is i%?

Example: Present value of 1 000$ to be received in 3 years if i = 10%?

PV = FV ¥ (P/F, i, n)
    = 1,000$ ¥ (P/F, 10%, 3)
    = 1,000$ ¥ 0.75131
PV = 751.31$

N	%i	PV	PMT	FV
3	10	?	0	1 000

Graphically, the discounting of a single amount looks like this:

Figure III.2

When dealing with non-annual conversions (in compounding or discounting) one must carefully adjust the periodic rate (entering the p_c rate, not the nominal annual rate) and the proper number of periods (entering **n** as conversion periods and not as years). This warning is mostly important for spreadsheet model building since HP calculator models do not require this precaution. Once the number of compounding periods has been chosen, you simply need to enter the nominal rate and the periodic rate will be computed directly.

2.3 The compounding of annuities

Annuities are regular streams of payments. Strictly speaking, an annuity should consist of payments made once annually, but the term also applies to any regular stream of monthly, quarterly or semiannual payments. In the symbolic formula, we use A = Annuity and reserve the notation PMT to the dollar amounts. Thus, the compounding of an annuity is written as:

$$(F/A, i, n) = \frac{(1+i)^n - 1}{i}$$

Example: If you deposit 100$ at the end of each year for 20 years to earn compound interest at 10% per annum, how much will you have on deposit at the end of the period?

FV = PMT ¥ (F/A, i, n)
   = 100$ ¥ (F/A, 10%, 20)
   = 100$ ¥ 57.2749
FV = 5,727.49$

N	%i	PV	PMT	FV
20	10	0	-100	?

Figure III.3

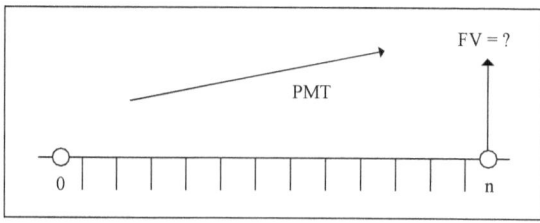

2.4 Discounting an annuity

This time we want to establish the present value of a stream of regular payments; that is we discount an annuity.

The discounting of an annuity is written:

$$(P/A, i, n) = \frac{1 - (1 + i)^{-n}}{i}$$

Example: what is the present value of 15,000$ to be received at the end of each year for 20 years if the annual interest rate is 10%?:

PV = PMT ¥ (P/A, i, n)
    = 15,000$ ¥ (P/A, 10%, 20)
    = 15,000$ ¥ 8.5135
PV = 127,703.46$

N	%i	PV	PMT	FV
20	10	?	-15000	0

Figure III.4

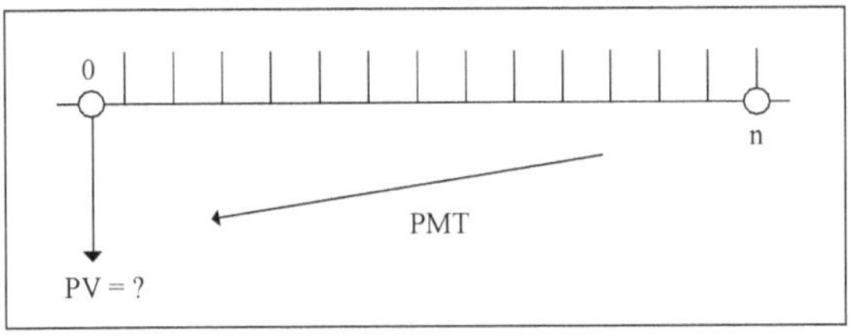

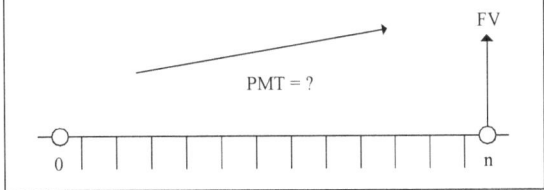

2.5 The sinking fund annuity

What would be the annuity required to built up a future amount of F over n periods if each deposit earns interest at the compound rate of i? The annuity factor allows us to solve this problem.

Graphically, a sinking fund accumulation resembles:

Figure III.5

And in its mathematical guise:

$$(A/F, i, n) = \frac{i}{(1 + i)^n - 1}$$

Example: what is the annuity required to accumulate 100,000$ in 30 years if annual deposits earn 10% per year?

INCOME PROPERTY ANALYSIS

$$PMT = FV ¥ (A/F, i, n)$$
$$= 100,000\$ ¥ (A/F, 10\%, 30)$$
$$= 100,000\$ ¥ 0.006079$$
$$PMT = 607.92\$$$

N	%i	PV	PMT	FV
30	10	0	?	100000

2.6 The amortisation factor

A present amount of PV $ can be depleted by regular withdrawal of annuities. A loan of PV $ will be similarly amortised over n periods if the rate of interest is i. Graphically, these equivalent problems can be portrayed as:

Figure III.6

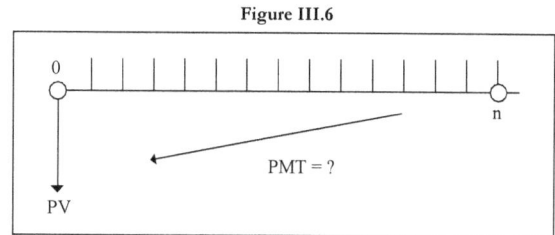

This amortisation factor (one of the most important for our purposes) is written:

$$(A/P, i, n) = \frac{i}{1 - (1 + i)^{-n}}$$

Example: what would a Property Professor's annual salary be (over 20 years) if it were financed by a 1,000,000$ one-time endowment earning 10% a year? (no hints intended)

$$PMT = PV ¥ (A/P, i, n)$$
$$= 1,000,000\$ ¥ (A/P, 10\%, 20)$$
$$= 1,000,000\$ ¥ (0.117460)$$
$$PMT = 117,459.62\$$$

N	%i	PV	PMT	FV
20	10	-1000000	?	0

For future reference, the reader may have the inclination to prove that:

$$(A/P, i, n) = i + (A/F, i, n)$$

The intuitive interpretation of this identity is that the annual repayment of a debt is made up partly of interest (i) and partly of a periodic repayment of some of the principal $(A/F, i, n)$ sufficient to reach the amount (FV) by the end of n periods and so dissolve the entire debt.

The following table condenses our six factors and its layout is meant to illustrate the intuitive and mathematical symmetry and reciprocity of these time factors.

Table III.3 The six time factors of one dollar

	Compounding →	Discounting ←
The time transformation of a single amount	$(F/P, i, n) = (1 + i)^n$	$(P/F, i, n) = \dfrac{1}{(1 + i)^n}$
The time transformation of an annuity	$(F/A, i, n) = \dfrac{(1 + i)^n - 1}{i}$	$(P/A, i, n) = \dfrac{1 - (1 + i)^{-n}}{i}$
The sinking fund and amortisation factors	$(A/F, i, n) = \dfrac{i}{(1 + i)^n - 1}$	$(A/P, i, n) = \dfrac{i}{1 - (1 + i)^{-n}}$

3. Varia: for further recycling

3.1 Perpetual annuities (or perpetuities)

Some bonds entitle the investor to a stream of fixed value coupons for an indefinite period: these are perpetual annuities whose value is readily found through a little manipulation of our initial $(P/A, i, n)$ formula:

$$(P/A, i, n) \underset{\longrightarrow \infty}{\text{when } n} = A \frac{1 - 1/(1 + i)^n}{i}$$

When n tends towards infinity, the $(1 + i)^n$ factor becomes very large and its inverse, $1/(1 + i)^n$, vanishes. Consequently, the perpetuity formula boils down to:

$$(P/A, i, n) \underset{\longrightarrow \infty}{\text{when } n} = A / i$$

Example: The present value of a perpetual annual dividend of 10 000$ bearing i = 15% is:

$$P = \frac{10,000 \$}{0.15} = 66,666.66 \$$$

The reader may be disappointed to realize that "eternity" is no big deal in financial matters since, for example, the present value of the same stream of dividends over 30 years hardly differs from the value of an infinite stream:

PV = 10,000 ¥ (P/A, 15%, 30)
PV = 65,659.79 $

This apparently minor digression will come in handy later...

3.2 Annuities due

So far our assumption has been that payments or deposits were made at the end of each period but we may be required to perform similar computations when payments or deposits are made at the beginning of each period: these beginning-of-the-period type of annuities are called annuities due. For example, rents are paid at the beginning of the month so this payment is compounded during the first month as illustrated below:

```
first month rent                                              last month rent
├ ─ ─ ─ ─ ─ ─ ─ + ─ ─ ─ ─ ─/+/─ ─ ─ + ─ ─ ─ ─ ─ ─ ─ ┤
beginning of         end of                              end of the
the month         the first month                       leasing period
```

The formulation must now take into account this extra compounding period:

PV = Rent ¥ (P/A , i , n) ¥ (1 + i)

Alternately, we could take the first month and add the discounted value of the n -1 following periods:

PV = First month rent + Rent ¥ (P/A , i , n -1)

Better yet, we can use the calculator's special choice of the BEGIN function.

In property analysis practice, by convention and for simplicity's sake, we choose to assume that rent and all other payments are made at the end of the period. Greater precision becomes futile given the shakiness of other information and hypotheses. Forecasting always means putting up with a fair deal of fuzziness.

3.3 Simple and general annuities[1]

Another assumption we have been entertaining is that conversion periods coincide exactly with payment periods. However, in some situations, the timing of conversions and payments may differ: these annuities are known as general annuities. Henceforth, **c** will stand for the number of conversion periods per year and **v** for the number of payments per year (**v** stands for *versement* = payment in French). Note that **c** can be greater or smaller than **v**.

Only when c = v (simple annuities) can we use the procedures outlined so far. Otherwise a distinct computation must be performed in order to obtain p_v the periodic rate per period of payment. (Recall: p_c is the periodic rate per period of conversion.)

Let's illustrate the case of a general annuity with monthly payments and semi-annual compounding (this quaint annuity is the most common way of calculating mortgage amortisation in Canada).

---

1. Non Canadian readers may skip this paragraph gleefully... except the last alinea of course.

In our notation, (A/P, p_v, n), one has to find the payment PMT required to amortise a debt PV whose repayment obeys a general annuity with parameters v = 12 and c = 2. The nominal rate can be expressed compactly using both indices:

$i_{c,v}$: Nominal rate with c conversions and v *versements* (payments)

For a Canadian mortgage one would write:

$i_{2,12}$: Nominal rate with semiannual conversion and monthly payments

To obtain the monthly rate p_v equivalent to the nominal rate $i_{c,v}$ you must equate the accumulation factors:

$(1 + p_v)^v = (1 + p_c)^c = (1 + i_{c,v}/c)^c$

And a little algebra gives us:

$p_v = \sqrt[v]{(1 + i_{c,v}/c)^c} - 1$

The monthly mortgage payment becomes:

$p_v = \sqrt[6]{(1 + i/2)} - 1$

This is the monthly rate which must be entered into the calculator to solve the formula (A/P, p_v, n). We can get p_V through various calculator routines, but we will use the quickest one in the demonstration that follows (with a nominal rate of $i_{2,12}$ = 15%).

Given a 1$ loan, a 15% rate compounded semiannually implies that 1.075$ [or (1 + 15%/2)] will be due at the end of the first semester. We could say that a "present" 1$ turns into a "future" 1.075$ in 6 months' time.

Figure III.7

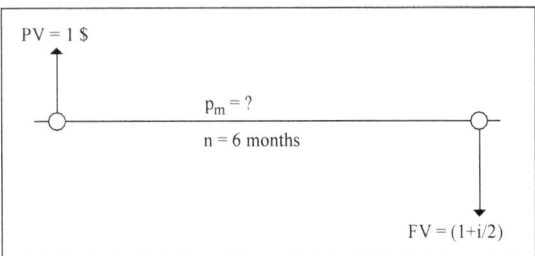

Given PV = 1$, FV = 1.075$ and n = 6 periods, we wish to extract the periodic rate that takes us from PV to FV in 6 periods. By exploiting our notation a little

differently (FV, PV and n are known but **i** is not) we have to solve for **i** in the Barata procedure.

N	%i	PV	PMT	FV
6	?	-1	0	1.075

With the proper value for i% stored in memory you can complete the calculation. If the loan were for an amount of 50,000$ amortised over 25 years, the monthly payment would be 623.07$.

It may be reassuring to know that Australian[1], Singaporean and Hong Kong mortgage payments are computed on the basis of monthly conversions and monthly payments (as in the US, Japan, Mexico, Indonesia, and most other countries in the world).

Thus such amortisations are based on simple annuities where the periodic rate is the twelfth of the nominal rate. Adapting the previous example ($i_{12,12}$) to the exigencies of a standard mortgage we find that:

PMT = PV ¥ (A/P, p, n)
    = 50,000$ ¥ (A/P, 15%/12, 300)
    = 50,000$ ¥ (A/P, 1.25%, 300)
PMT = 640.41$

4. Present value, net present value and internal rate of return

We now have all the Lego blocks needed to assemble the most useful of the analyst's tools. Let's proceed step by step.

4.1 The present value of two amounts

• What is the present worth of 1,000$ receivable in one year and of 1,500$ to be received in 2 years if the discount rate is $i_{1,1} = 10\%$?

Mathematically we could write:

PV = $FV_1/(1+i)^1$ + $FV_2/(1+i)^2$
   = $1,000\$/(1+0.10)^1$ + $1,500\$/(1+0.10)^2$
   = 909.09$ + 1,239.67$
PV = 2,148.76$

---

1. Actually, not quite. The Australian mortgage amortisation system is quite bizarre and will be discussed in chapter IV.

Figure III.8

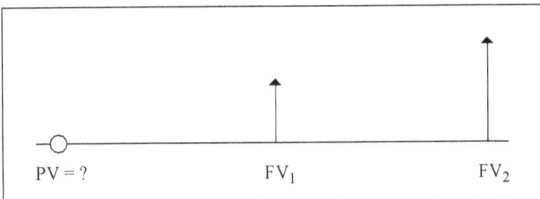

• What is the present value of an 800$ investment returning 1,000$ at the years end if the discount rate is 10%?

Suppose the 800$ investment is made at the beginning of the year and the promised 1,000$ is due at the very end. By convention, negative amounts (outlays) are represented by a downward pointing arrow whereas positive amounts (incomes) are represented by an upward pointing arrow. Our little story can be depicted as:

Figure III.9

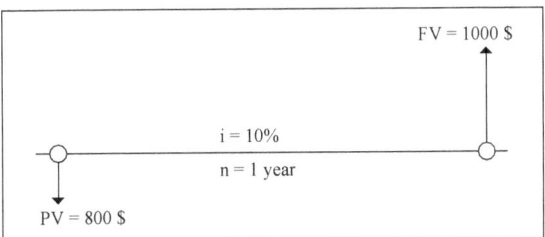

The initial investment is not discounted but regarded as a negative input:

PV   = - 800$ + 1,000$/(1+ i)^1
PV   = - 800$ + 909.09$
PV   = 109.09$

The result is called the **Net Present Value** (NPV) of the investment. This is the most important concept in investment analysis: simple but crucial.

4.2 The internal rate of return

We can immediately press the key IRR and wait to get the result 25.00 after a few seconds. This is the internal rate of return on our 800$: the discount rate which equates the present value of the year end 1000$ income with the current outlay of 800$. In other words, it is the discount rate that reduces the investment's net present value to naught.

N	%i	PV	PMT	FV
1	?	-800	0	1000

In our very simple story, we could have asked:

FV = PV $(1 + i?)^1$

1 000$ = 800$ $(1 + i?)^1$

Or symbolically:

1000$ = 800$ (P/F , i? ,1)

Figure III.10

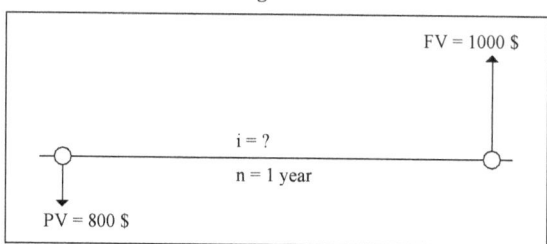

In this form, it becomes apparent that the internal rate of return is that discount rate which satisfies the identity. The calculator reacts sluggishly when computing an IRR (in more complex cases it may take several seconds to obtain the result); in fact the machine iterates: it proceeds through trial and error, testing different discount rates and checking whether the result is positive, negative or null. Once it has homed in very close to zero, it stops and displays the closest approximation of the internal rate of return.

Let's mull over our results. The 10% discount rate has given us a net present value of 109.09$. That is, the investor earns a return of 10% on his investment and an extra 109.09$ to boot: his wealth has increased by 109.09$. Had the net present value been exactly equal to zero, his return would have been exactly 10%, as would the internal rate of return. In the present example, the net present value is positive, indicating that the return is greater than 10%: we already know that his return is 25%. We should keep this reasoning in mind until we return later to measuring investment returns.

4.3 Present value, internal rate and annuities

• What is the net present value (given a 10% discount rate) and the internal rate of return of a 10,000$ loan calling for 10 annual payments of 1,500$?

To the lender, this loan would consist of an outlay (the 10,000$ loaned) followed by a stream of income (1,500$ per year for 10 years).

Figure III.11

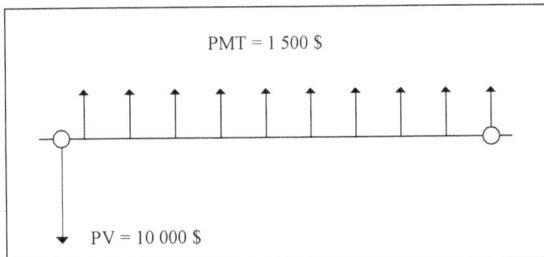

To obtain the net present value, we simply have to solve the following equation where the initial (negative) investment is added to the present value of an annuity of 1 500$ over 10 years at a rate of 10%:

NPV? = -10 000 $ + 1 500 $ × $\dfrac{1-(1+0.10)^{-10}}{0.10}$

To get to the internal rate of return we solve for IRR:

10 000 $ = 1 500 $ × $\dfrac{1-(1+IRR?)^{-10}}{IRR?}$

Or, consistent with our notation:

NPV? = - PV   +   PMT ¥ (P/A , i , n)
     = - 10,000$ +   1,500$ ¥ (P/A , 0.10 , 10)
     = - 783.15$

N	%i	PV	PMT	FV
10	?	-10000	1500	0

And the IRR (i%) will be 8.14%.

• What is the net present value (at a discount rate of 10%) and the internal rate of return on a loan of 10,000$ refundable by 10 annual payments of 1,500$ and a final "balloon" (a single extra payment) of 3,000$? Now the picture would be:

Figure III.12

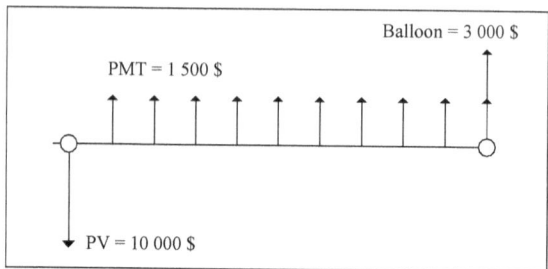

This time the equation is a bit more complex. We add the initial investment of -10 000$; then the present value of the 1 500$ 10 year annuity and, finally, the present value of the 3 000$ to be received at the end of 10 years:

$$\text{NPV?} = -10\,000\,\$ + 1\,500\,\$ \times \frac{1-(1+0.10)^{-10}}{0.10} + 3\,000\,\$ \times (1+0.10)^{-10}$$

And the IRR equation is now:

$$10\,000\,\$ = 1\,500\,\$ \times \frac{1-(1+i?)^{-10}}{i?} + 3\,000\,\$(1+i?)^{-10}$$

Our notation allows us to express this more elegantly as:

NPV? = - PV + PMT ¥ (P/A, i, n) + FV ¥ (P/F, i, n)
= - 10,000$ + 1,500$ (P/A, 0.10, 10) + 3,000$ (P/F, 0.10, 10)
= - 783.14$ + 1,156.63$
NPV? = 373.48$

To find the IRR we write and solve:

PV = PMT ¥ (P/A, i?, n) + FV ¥ (P/F, i?, n)
10,000$ = 1,500$ (P/A, i?, n) + 3,000$ (P/F, i?, n)

On the calculator, we know four of the variables and we need to find the fifth:

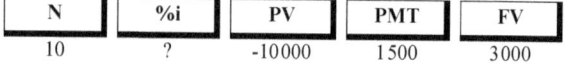

N	%i	PV	PMT	FV
10	?	-10000	1 500	3 000

And the resulting IRR is 10.77%.

We can even double check our definition of the IRR: the rate for which the net present value equals zero. If we do discount the previous stream of payments at 10.77%, we will obtain a NPV equal to zero. And, to make sure, we may recompute the net present value at a rate of 10%. The resulting net present value will indeed be 373.48 $.

• Now we are all set to describe any investment as an initial outlay of (V_0) followed by a stream of expenditures or revenues (A_t) and, eventually, the disposition of the asset (V_n). The investment could as well be a building, a dam, a hospital or a space shuttle.

Figure III.13

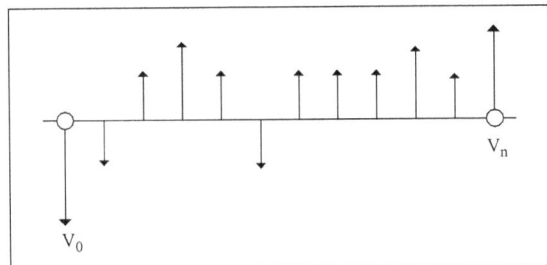

The following equations symbolise the information contained in Table III.4:

$$NPV = -V_0 - \frac{A_1}{(1+i)^1} - \frac{A_2}{(1+i)^2} + \frac{A_3}{(1+i)^3} + \frac{A_4}{(1+i)^4} + \frac{V_5}{(1+i)^5}$$

$$NPV = -V_0 - A_1 (P/F, i, 1) - A_2 (P/F, i, 2) + A_3 (P/F, i, 3) + A_4 (P/F, i, 4) + V_5 (P/F, i, 5)$$

Table III.4 The NPV and IRR of the Tertius project

Years		Expenses and incomes	Discount factor (for a rate of 12%)	Present value at 12%
0	V_0	- 8000	$(1 + 0.12)^{-0} = 1.00$	- 8,000.00 $
1	A_1	- 500	$(1 + 0.12)^{-1} = 0.89$	- 446.43 $
2	A_2	- 200	$(1 + 0.12)^{-2} = 0.79$	- 159.44 $
3	A_3	800	$(1 + 0.12)^{-3} = 0.71$	569.42 $
4	A_4	100	$(1 + 0.12)^{-4} = 0.69$	63.55 $
5	V_n	17,000	$(1 + 0.12)^{-5} = 0.63$	9,646.26 $
Net present value				1,673.36 $
Internal rate of return				16.23 %

This table can be constructed step by step using the calculator as outlined here, or preferably, with the help of the NPV and IRR keys. When computations become more complex, it is much wiser to use spreadsheets offering NPV and IRR functions. The IPAV Excel workbook provides both manual and "function" calculations in order to facilitate the transition from "calculators" to computers. The reader should feel **very** comfortable with these exercises before proceeding further.

5. Practical conclusion

The rest of this textbook will be hard to follow if these basic financial maths notions, the use of financial calculators, and basic spreadsheet skills are not under total control.

The IPA website provides all the required computational crutches: Excel tables, Excel financial functions, a tutorial on how to use your calculator and a complete Menu for computer laboratories practices.

Chapter IV

Property financing

Where we learn the mechanics of mortgage analysis, introduce some useful applications and take a glimpse at the less than transparent Australian mortgage instruments.

Property investors thrive on debt. Any real estate project, from its birth to its demise, is bred and fed on borrowed funds. Given the size and the perennial nature of most investment projects, property financing relies heavily on long term debt instruments such as mortgage loans or mortgage bonds. This chapter is chiefly devoted to the study of traditional mortgage instruments even though the panoply of financing tools is much richer and growing in diversity.

The most common way of financing property is through mortgage contracts with the property's value put up as collateral for the loan. This close relationship linking the value, the asset and the amount of financing explains why the financing decision is so intimately related to the investment decision and why, by contrast with the treatment usually advocated by corporate finance analysts, our fundamental decision model (the 'equity model') will explicitly account for the cost of financing.

The tools and underpinnings of the mortgage market are quite complex and diversified, and are further obfuscated by a thick layer of jargon and technicalities. We will only skim the surface of this domain and limit our concern to the elements of mortgage *cuisine i.e.,* the basic calculations needed to set up amortisation schedules and conduct the simplest form of mortgage valuation. However elementary these techniques may appear, regretfully, we are reminded daily how poorly they are understood, even by professional lenders or investors:

— For example, pre-calculated mortgage tables are still widely used even though they are totally inappropriate for most realistic mortgage calculations.

— We witness the frequent misinterpretation, and hence miscalculation, of loan interest adjustments, balances outstanding and, obviously, the realistic evaluation of a mortgage contract's true cost. In particular, the atypical Australian amortisation system is very poorly understood and - once again

- creates major difficulties when using standard calculators and Excel functions.
— Finally we must concede that we still do not fully grasp how financing and refinancing affect the value of properties; we will address this vexing issue more fully in the appendix of Chapter VI.

1. Paying back a loan

Property loans can be quite complex legal and financial instruments of various forms and conditions. A typical loan contract must be described by the following minimum set of characteristics and conditions (covenants):

- rate of interest
- length of the reimbursement period
- frequency and composition of the payments
- initial and carrying charges
- prepayment conditions and penalties
- refinancing options and conditions
- nature of guarantees
- resolution and foreclosure conditions

These various conditions will influence the effective cost of a loan and its management. This chapter will only describe the most basic forms of loan repayments.

1.1 Interest-only loans

The simplest form of repayment consists in periodic payments of interests applied to the full value of the loan.

Example:

An interest-only loan mortgage is written for 100,000.00$ with a nominal rate of $i = 8\%$ and must be repaid at the end of the year. Interests must be paid monthly.

The monthly rate is:

$p_m = 8\%/12 = 0.6666\%$

The monthly payment is:

PMT   =   PV × p_m

666.66 $ =   100,000 $ × 0.6666%

The outstanding balance at the end of the loan will thus be:

OSB = PV = 100,000 $

Such loans are still used for short term loans, vendor financing and construction loans. They are not suitable for longer period loans since most of the default risk is borne by the lender.

1.2 Amortised fixed-rate loans

Amortisation is the process of liquidating debt over time or, if you prefer, 'killing' debt; in the word 'amortisation', you find the root *mort* (death in French). In most countries mortgage loans are amortised with uniform, blended payments compounded monthly and payable at the end of the month. The characteristics of our system can be so summarized:

— the monthly payment is constant and made up of principal and interest (blended payment);

— the monthly payment is made at the end of each period;

— the compounding of interest is performed on a monthly basis.

Our first objective is to round up all the elements needed to set up a proper amortisation table, namely: the monthly payment; the split between interest and principal for each blended monthly payment; the balance outstanding on the loan and the last payment.

The monthly rate and the monthly payment

To compute the monthly charge, we must first determine the appropriate monthly rate of interest. Since, in most other countries, we have a monthly payment and monthly compounding, the monthly rate is simply equal to the annual nominal rate divided by 12.

Example:

A mortgage is written for 100,000.00$ with a nominal rate of $i = 8\%$ and a 10 year amortisation period.

The monthly rate is $p_m = 8\%/12 = 0.6666\%$.

The rest of the procedure is based on the 'Barata' calculation of the payment:

N	%i	PV	PMT	FV
120	0.6666	100,000	?	0

The exact payment would be 1,213.275944 $ (rounded up to 1,213.28$).

This annuity will amortise the full amount of the loan. But, the composition of the equal payments of 1,213.28$ does not remain constant. In an amortised loan, from one month to the other, interest makes up a decreasing portion of the annuity since it is computed on a declining balance outstanding. The rest of the payment is composed of principal reimbursement and contributes to the monthly reduction of the balance outstanding (figure IV.1).

Figure IV.1

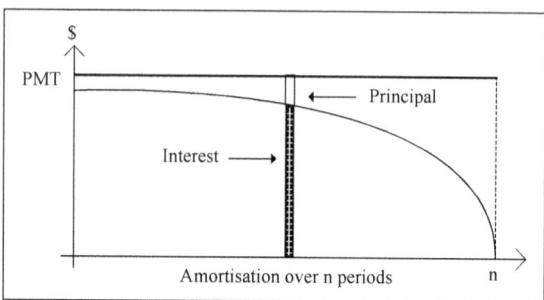

The periodic split between interest and principal

Each t period's monthly blended payment is made up partly of interest (INT_t) and partly of the recovery of the borrowed capital (RC_t):

PMT = $INT_t + RC_t$

Monthly interest is calculated on the balance outstanding of the previous month (OSB_{t-1}), we write:

INT_t = $OSB_{t-1} \times p_m$

INT_t : Interest due in month t

OSB_{t-1} : Outstanding balance at the end of the previous period

p_m : Monthly rate

The recovery of the principal (or capital) is simply inferred by subtracting the interest from the amount of the payment:

RC_t = PMT - INT_t

The results can be obtained with the specific menu for amortisation on the HP calculator and most similar models.

Monthly split between interest and principal (in Dollars)

Month	Payment	Interest	Principal
1	1,213.28	667.67	546.61
2	1,213.28	663.02	550.26
3	1,213.28	659.35	553.93
4	1,213.28	655.66	557.62
5	1,213.28	651.94	561.34
6	1,213.28	648.20	565.08
...	...	...	...

It would be useful to obtain not only the monthly INT/RC split but also the total amounts paid over many periods. For example, we may need to know the amount of interest paid yearly on a loan since this interest is deductible from income.

The naive solution to this problem would be to multiply the monthly interest by 12, but the reader knows better and she won't fall into this trap. She knows that the interest portion of the loan decreases from one month to the next and that, consequently, we must use the appropriate interval periods in the amortisation menus. Thus, for example, to obtain the interests accumulated during the second year, one must ask for the accumulation between month 13 and 24.

Outstanding balance

Mortgage loans can be amortised over long periods (10 to 30 years) and the contractual conditions remain the same for the entire period. More recent forms of loans are still amortised on a long period, but they may be due and payable at the end of a much shorter term (typically 1, 3, or 5 years). Come the end of the term, the balance outstanding must be either reimbursed, refinanced with another lender or rolled over with the same lender. In any event, the conditions and even the amount of the loan are liable to be modified at the end of each term. From now on, we will note **t** the length of the term and **n** the amortisation period.

> Australian financial institutions use the expression 'term' to describe the amortisation period (n). Right or wrong, this usage creates a confusion in most borrowers' minds.
>
> > The **term** is when the mortgage 'terminates', thus when the borrower pays back his loan.
> >
> > The **amortisation** is the theoretical amount of time that would be required to pay back the full amount. Most mortgages 'terminate' well before they fully amortised.
>
> Let's keep in mind:
>
> > t for term (for terminate)
> >
> > n for amortisation (for 'mort' = dead)
> >
> > and most of the time: t < n

Generally we may also have to calculate the balance outstanding on a loan for many reasons (disposition of the property, full repayment before the term expires, foreclosure, preparation of a balance sheet, etc.) and we should be in a position to quote the balance outstanding at any given point of the amortisation schedule.

Routinely published mortgage tables are useless to us in performing this task, especially when one has to deal with real life situations which typically involve omitted or delayed payments, refinancing or accelerated reimbursement. Again your calculator will be helpful when faced with these common problems. Every financial calculator is different thus you may need to read the user's guide.

A shortcut solution to find the OSB: the 'FV' function key

This useful shortcut will be demonstrated here with our old friend 'la Barata'.

— The first step is used to compute the payment over the full amortisation:

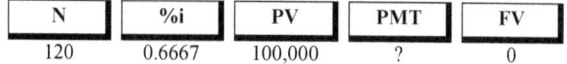

N	%i	PV	PMT	FV
120	0.6667	100,000	?	0

— And, in the second step, the term is keyed in (here 36 months).

The resulting **FV** is of course the outstanding balance.

NOTE: EXCEL

In Excel you compute the outstanding balance by calculating:

Balance = Loan - Cumulated principal.

The cumulated principal is calculated with the function CUMPRINC. This function requires the 'Analysis Toolpak' (Tool>>Add-in>>Analysis Toolpak). Note also that the CUMPRINC function is capricious: the loan cannot be entered as negative and you must scroll down the menu to enter type = 0).

The amortisation schedule

We are now fully equipped to build the complete amortisation table of our 10 year, 100,000$ loan, bearing a nominal rate $i_{12,12}$ of 8%. The complete procedure is now displayed *in extenso* for the last time.

Table IV.1 The Partial Amortisation Table (in dollars)

Years	Months	Payments	Interest	Principal	Balance
0	0	0	0	0	100,000.00
1	1	1213.28	666.67	546.61	99,453.39
	2	1213.28	663.02	550.26	98,903.13
	3	1213.28	659.35	553.93	98,349.20
...	...	...	...	...	...
	71	1213.28	342.96	870.32	50,573.85
6	72	1213.28	337.16	876.12	49,697.73
...	...	...	...	...	...
	119	1213.28	16.01	1,197.27	1204.51
10	120	1213.28	8.03	1,205.25	0.00*

* In fact, because of the rounding up of the monthly payments, the final balance will not be exactly equal to zero ... it will be negative since monthly payments are slightly too large ... we will neglect this rounding up effect for the moment.

When required — for tax reasons for example — the annual table could also be drawn up:

Table IV.2 Annual summary of a $(100{,}000\$, i = 8\%, n = 120$ months) loan amortisation

Years	Interest	Principal	Balance
0			100,000.00 $
1	7 754.06 $	6 805.30 $	93 194.70 $
2	7 189.23 $	7 370.13 $	85 824.57 $
3	6 577.51 $	7 981.85 $	77 842.72 $
4	5 915.02 $	8 644.34 $	69 198.39 $
5	5 197.55 $	9 361.81 $	59 836.57 $
6	4 420.52 $	10 138.84 $	49 697.73 $
7	3 579.00 $	10 980.36 $	38 717.37 $
8	2 667.64 $	11 891.72 $	26 825.65 $
9	1 680.63 $	12 878.73 $	13 946.92 $
10	611.70 $	13 947.66 $	-0.74 $
Total		100,000.00 $	

1.3 The variable rate amortised loan

Fixed interest loans can create financing risks for the lenders and borrowers. Now such loans are limited to shorter periods (1 to 5 years) and the residential mortgage market is increasingly relying on variable rates. Some new mortgage cocktails may even cover fixed amounts combined with variable parts, or even varying variable parts of the loan.

Typically the timing and rates of variations seem to be left to the discretion of the lenders and the conditions and transparency of the computations are, to say the least, very opaque for most borrowers.

A simple and limited example is presented below. The rates are modified at any time during the year and the new monthly rate is applied to the outstanding balance and the loan is amortised on the residual term. Most variable rates schemes are based on this amortise-as-you-go treatment of monthly payments.

$$PMT_t = OSB_{t-1} \times (A/P, i_v, n - (t-1))$$

Our 100,000 $ loan (n = 120 months) with a variable rate would be amortised as described below. For example, the third month payment would be written:

$$PMT_3 = OSB_2 \times (A/P, 6.8\%/12, 120 - (3-1)), \text{etc.}$$

You may need to draw a monthly time line to get this right!

Needless to say that the standard functions of a financial calculator cannot be used to write such a table... unless you are very patient. A spreadsheet or some other form of software is almost indispensable to track such a loan.

Table IV.3 A plain vanilla variable mortgage table... 1st year

Month	Annual rates	PMT	INT	PRINC	OSB
1	6.5	1,135.48	541.67	593.81	99,406.19
2	6.6	1,140.54	546.74	593.80	98,812.39
3	6.8	1,150.62	559.94	590.68	98,221.71
4	6.4	1,130.66	523.85	606.81	97,614.90
5	6.5	1,135.60	528.75	606.85	97,008.05
6	6.9	1,155.30	557.80	597.50	96,410.55
7	6.5	1,135.74	522.23	613.51	95,797.04
8	6.5	1,135.74	518.91	616.83	95,180.21
9	6.5	1,135.74	515.56	620.18	94,560.03
10	6.7	1,145.27	527.97	617.30	93,942.73
11	6.8	1,150.02	532.35	617.67	93,325.06
12	6.9	1,154.73	536.62	618.11	92,706.95
...	...	...	...	...	...

2. The Australian mortgage (Platypus format ...[1])

Australian financial institutions amortise mortgages in a unique way that combine simple annuities repayments and daily summation of interest.

For residential mortgages the most common options are monthly, fortnightly or weekly periodicities. Thus, compounding (c) and payments (v) frequencies can be monthly, fortnightly or weekly. According to our notations, nominal rates and periodic rates could be written:

Table IV.4

Periodicity	Nominal rates	Periodic rates
	$i_{c,v}$	pc
Monthly	$i_{12,12}$	$pm = i_{12,12}/12$
Fortnightly	$i_{26,26}$	$pft = i_{26,26}/26$
Weekly	$i_{52,52}$	$pw = i_{52,52}/52$

---

1. The platypus (Ornithorhynchus anatinus) is considered to be one of the world's most unusual animals. It is often described as a living fossil - a furry, warm-blooded, egg-laying mammal that retains some features of reptiles. This specie of egg-laying mammal is uniquely Australian, and – for the analogy – as bizarre as an Australian mortgage with monthly compounding and daily summing of interests.

Thus depending on the periodicity, the periodic payments can be computed as simple annuities by using the financial calculator (or Excel functions) and adjusting the number of compounding periods (P/Yr) to 12, 26 or 52 periods.

Unfortunately, the calculator (and Excel functions) cannot be used directly to compute the periodic interests, principal and outstanding balances because of the way interests are computed.

Generally the Australian mortgage interests are computed at a daily rate, applied to the latest outstanding balance and kept constant until the end of the period.

For example, for a weekly amortisation, the payments are computed normally as $(A/P, p_w, n * 52)$ and paid at the end of the week. The interest charged will be the sum of daily interest computed as $OSB * (i/365)$ and the principal is computed as:

$$PRIN_w = PMT_w - INT_w$$

$$PRIN_w = PMT_w - \text{Sum of } INT_{daily}$$

$$PRIN_w = PMT_w - \text{Sum of } (OSB_w\text{-}1 * i/365)$$

Almost as bizarre as a Platypus, the Australian mortgage is a mix of 'normal' simple compounding and daily computing and summation of interests.

The following example should clarify the procedure.

Table IV.5 A platypus mortgage: basic information

Loan	P	100 000.00 $
nominal rate	inom	10.00%
conversions	c_	52
number of days per year	ndy	365
daily interest rate	pc	0.0273973%
number of payments	v	52
amortisation in years	n	30
applicable rate per week	pw	0.1923%
effective rate	ie	10.5065%
(A/P , i , n)	factor	0.002024144
weekly payment	PMT	202.41 $

Day	PMT	INT	PRINC	Daily OSB
				100,000.00 $
01/01/2002	0.00 $	27.40 $	0.00 $	100,027.40 $
02/01/2002	0.00 $	27.40 $	0.00 $	100,054.79 $
03/01/2002	0.00 $	27.40 $	0.00 $	100,082.19 $
04/01/2002	0.00 $	27.40 $	0.00 $	100,109.59 $
05/01/2002	0.00 $	27.40 $	0.00 $	100,136.99 $
06/01/2002	0.00 $	27.40 $	0.00 $	100,164.38 $
07/01/2002	202.41 $	27.40 $	0.00 $	100,191.78 $
07/01/2002	202.41 $	191.78 $	10.63 $	99,989.37 $

There is nothing inherently wrong with this 'Platypus mortgage' except that standard computations required for mortgage analysis are more difficult to perform since they require modifications of calculator or Excel standard functions.

Since we concentrate on commercial properties - we will neglect the 'Platypus' types of complications and we will assume that we deal with 'standard' mortgages based on regular monthly amortisation and compounding interests. This 'standard' method is the one that allows you to use your financial calculator and Excel financial functions. And, since we deal here with property investment we should not be concerned with the small errors that can result from such a simplication.

In the Pacific Islands the regular amortisation method ($i_{12,12}$) is applied. So, don't worry too much and you can rely on your financial calculators and Excel functions.

3. Applications

3.1 The effective cost of a mortgage loan

The real cost of a mortgage is always greater than the nominal rate announced by the lender. The difference between the nominal rate and the real cost is due to three combined effects: the conversion effect, the 'padding effect' and the 'clouding effect'.

• The conversion effect

We already know that a shorter conversion period leads to a higher effective rate. The effective rate can be obtained using the one dollar factor approach (PV = 1, FV = 1 + i/c, c and p?) or more directly with the ICONV menu.

As an illustration of the conversion effect, let us compute the effective rate on our 8% nominal rate:

$$1 + i_{effective} = (1 + 0.08/12)^{12} = 1.082299951$$

$i_{effective}$ = 8.23%

• The 'padding' effect

The effective cost of a mortgage contract is also increased thanks to the sundry charges and conditions added to the deal. For example, loan establishment fees, valuation fees, loan insurance premiums, in line fees and prepayment penalties are included in most contracts and these extra elements contribute to pad the cost by a few percentage points. Let us try to measure this padding effect on the 100,000$ contract signed between Mr. Borough and Ms. Highlender.

A fully amortised (100,000$, $i_{12,12}$ = 8%, n = 10 years) loan calls for a 500$ establishment fee and a 1% insurance premium paid up front. In line management fees of 15$ are levied monthly and, finally, the borrower will have to pay a 2 month interest prepayment penalty. This penalty is meant to compensate Ms. Highlender for the fact that an early prepayment may not be reinvested readily at the same attractive yield.

In this case, Mr. Borough does reimburse the full outstanding amount by the end of the third year and we want to find Mr. Borough's borrowing cost and Ms. Highlender's effective yield.

To solve this very general problem, we write the equivalence between the amount effectively received by Mr. Borough at the beginning of the contract (noted PV*) and the stream of payments made during the 36 month period and at the end of the last month. The rate for which this equation holds is the effective rate we are seeking. Let's review the different components of our analysis:

— In effect, Mr. Borough does not receive the full value of PV = 100,000$ but only PV* = 98,500$ because the 500$ establishment fee and the 1,000$ insurance premium are substracted up front:

PV* = PV - 'all the up front goodies'

— The management monthly fee of 15$ will be added to the regular payments and the prepayment penalty is computed as 2 times the interest of the last month (the 36th):

Effective loan:	PV*	= 100,000 - 500 - 1,000 = 98,500$
Monthly charge:	PMT	= 100,000 (A/P , i , n) + monthly fee
		= 733.77 + 15 = 748.77$
Penalty:	Penalty	= INT_{36} × 2 = 1,298.20$
Outstanding balance:	OSB_{36}	= 97,122.40$

— We could write the equivalence (in dollars):

98,500 = 748.77 (P/A , **i?** , 36) + 1,298.20 (P/F , **i?** , 36) + 97,122.40 (P/F , **i?** , 36)

98,500 = 748.77 (P/A , **i ?**, 36) + (1,298.20 + 97,122.40) × (P/F , **i?** , 36)

— The rate which solves this equation is nothing other than the Internal Rate of Return. In this case, the result will be nominal rate of 9.14% and thus an effective annual rate of 9,54% ... a bit heavier than our initial advertised rate of 8%!

The padding effect would be even more significant on a shorter period. For instance, given identical conditions, the effective rate would reach 11.81% if the term of the loan were reduced to one year (try it as an exercise...). This can be explained by the fact that the fixed costs (establishment fees and insurance premium) are amortised on a shorter period and also because the prepayment penalty is more severe at the beginning of the loan when interest represents a greater proportion of the monthly charge.

The following table illustrates a typical schedule of 'padding' expenses for an Australian simple residential mortgage in 2002 (on a loan of 100,000 $ and loan to value ratio of 90%).

Lending expenses		
Establishment fees	$	600.00
Mortgage registration/title search	$	88.00
Stamp duties on mortgage document	$	347.50
Stamp duties on duplicate	$	5.00
Valuation fees	$	200.00
Construction progress inspection fees	$	-
Lenders mortgage insurance	$	1,130.00
Other lending related expenses	$	85.00
Lending related cost total	$	2,455.50
Total related expenses	**$**	**7,140.86**

• The 'clouding' effect

And everything gets even fuzzier when one ponders the many possible means a lender can find to increase or protect his yield.

— We have already some of the various bells and whistles attached to residential mortgages. These additional elements complexify the computation of effective costs and increase the general cloud of suspicion harboured by residential borrowers

— For mortgages on commercial properties, the lender may levy a certain share of the building's net or gross operating income (participating mortgages);

— The lender could also negotiate a very advantageous rental contract in the office or commercial building he finances (sweet leasing terms);

— He may also wish to hold equity benefits in the form of shares in the developer's company, or in the form of a land leaseback arrangement, or as a percentage share of the property's added value upon resale. Many such 'equity kickers' are developed routinely for commercial lending activities. The concept had even been applied to the residential market with Shared Appreciation Mortgages (SAMs) in the US when mortgage rate where very high. This idea has recently being resurrected in Australia (In 2003). This resurrection does not make much sense when - historically - mortgage rates have never been so low. If it were applied, this imported concept would certainly lead to major public relation headaches for mortgage lenders.

These diverse terms and conditions of a loan make for a cloudy picture of the 'true' cost of the loan and make it almost impossible to compare different alternative mortgage contracts.

4. Practical conclusion

This chapter may appear quite technical but it does cover concepts and procedures which are the basis of most property transactions. Unfortunately, these instruments are not always clearly understood by consumers, investors and, oddly enough, not even by lenders.

We should also reassure the reader since - as stated previously - we will safely ignore most of the mortgage complication for the rest of this textbook. In the following examples and attached software, we will assume that mortgages are amortised normally (monthly payments, compounded interests) and are not burdened by various additional bells and whistles. The loss of accuracy should not bother a realistic investment analyst.

Chapter V

Elements of property taxation

Where the basic rules of property taxation are presented and illustrated. Where we also learn to be suspicious of the appeal of apparent tax shelters.

Caveat 1:

It is always risky to even try to summarise fiscal legislation. The tax laws are complex, forever changing and of the utmost importance to the property investor. Only the basic rules are presented here and the reader would be well advised to never overestimate his newly acquired expertise; he should always seek professional assistance for real-life investment decision making.

Caveat 2:

Fiscal texts are particularly short-lived. They have to be modified after every new budget and this warning is particularly opportune at the time of this writing since we are in the midst of a major wave of fiscal changes in Australia and in many South-East Asia Countries. This chapter is intentionally general in scope and readers should periodically check the IPA website to observe how the taxation winds are shifting.

Caveat 3:

Fiscal considerations are crucial to any and all property decisions, but they should never be the only motivation. It is usually a costly error to judge an investment on the sole basis of its tax sheltering ability. In the early 1990s, many 'negatively geared' property investors were mulling over this common bit of financial wisdom. However investors seem to have a very short memory and quite a few seem to be attracted to the same traps in recent years.

The effects of taxation are essential to the property analyst since she is solely concerned with the measurement of after-tax cash flows. Conversely, the valuer should, in principle, limit his analysis to the measurement of net incomes (operating and disposal income before-debt and before-tax). In reality, tax considerations are implicit in the proper treatment of capitalisation techniques, thus the valuer must command a thorough understanding of the taxation factors affecting the very market he must constantly monitor and analyse.

Taxation regulations and their interpretations are complex since the 'Australian Income Tax Assessment Act' recognizes and treats many types of incomes and taxpayers differently. For example, capital gains are fully taxed in the hands of 'professional' property investors (those in the business of trading properties for gains), partially taxed in the hands of most others and totally exempt when an owner disposes of his principal residence. And finally, choosing a form of ownership (individual ownership, partnerships, trusts and companies) may also lead to quite different fiscal and property decisions.[1]

The property analyst must also have some idea of the owner's income from other sources to apply the proper marginal taxation rate to operating and disposal taxable income. It may be useful to restate the obvious... but properties as such are never taxed, only their owners or owning entities are. That's why, beyond the subject property, the rest of the fiscal picture also matters.

Table V.1 illustrates the taxpayer categories and the different forms of income subject to taxation.

Table V.1 Taxpayers and sources of income

Types of ownership status:
- Personal ownership
    . a sole owner
    . joint tenant or tenants-in-common
    . partners
- Corporate ownership
    . private companies
    . public companies
    . cooperative or mutual funds
- Trust Ownership
    . family or discretionary trust
    . investment trust

Types of income (when analysing properties):
    . from recurrent income
    . from capital gain on disposal
    . from all other sources

---

1. For example, partners pay tax on partnership income, whereas companies pay tax which reduces the tax to be paid by shareholders. At the time of writing, the Treasurer has announced plans to tax trusts in future as if they are companies.

This chapter will deal chiefly with the taxation of individual taxpayers deriving income from a property investment.

Consistent with previous chapters, we will again carefully distinguish between an investment's time sequence (acquisition, operation and disposition) and discuss the fiscal treatment of each level.

Most of this chapter will be devoted to the Commonwealth (The Australian Tax Office: ATO) taxation of property revenues and profits. However property is taxed from other sources. The full range of sequenced taxes and tax menus are described in the IPA website.

State and local government taxes being 'local' will not be discussed here. They are fully presented, illustrated and calculated in the IPA website. Since various rates and conditions are modified quite frequently readers should check their website periodically.

The treatment of GST is also relegated to the website again to make sure that the reader has access to the latest information concerning this very shifty piece of tax headache.

1. Taxing operating income

Regular and occasional income from any property are assessable and added to the taxpayer other forms of income during the fiscal year that they are received. For a given year, operating incomes can be regular rents, recovery of expenses from tenants, proceeds from vending or washing machines, interests on property related deposits, compensation for lost rent, retained rental bond money, letting fees, special functions rentals, etc. For the same given year, a variety of deductions can reduce the assessable income from the property.

A taxpayer who owns more than one property (a portfolio of properties or shares of properties) will accumulate all the net assessable incomes (all incomes reduced by all allowable expenditures).

Beyond this simple principle, some important issues must be solved in order to establish the proper level of taxable operating income.

1.1 Operation or capital expenditures?

Is an expense deductible during the year or treated as a capital expenditure used to increase the value of the asset? The difference does matter since a deductible expense provides a tax deduction immediately, whereas a capitalised expenditure may only provide a tax advantage at the time of disposal (to be clarified later...).

• A property's ordinary operating expenditures are entirely deductible in the tax year in which they are incurred and reduce the investor's taxable income. These expenditures must be normal maintenance, operating and management expenses, such as (but not limited to):

- property rates: council rates, water rates, land tax;
- insurance premiums (building, content, liability, mortgage);
- servicing contracts;
- heating and electricity;
- pest control;
- travel expenses (related to management of the property);
- current legal, management and leasing fees;
- wages and related expenditures;
- ground rents, head rent;
- tenants incentives (not of a capital nature);
- advertising costs;
- prepaid expenses (normally deducted in the year of payment);
- bank charges;
- interest on loans.

• Repairs and maintenance of plant and buildings are normally treated as current expenditures as long as they do not substantially increase the value or change the nature of the asset. By contrast, improvement expenditures are treated as being capital in nature and thus not deductible in the year. The zone separating repairs from improvement is a tax lawyer paradise since the line can be quite thin and open to argumentation. It is generally in the taxpayer's best interest to deduct (now) than to capitalise (later) but when an expenditures cannot be deducted it will be treated as a capital expenditure.

• Capital expenditures encompass those incurred in acquiring an asset or increasing its value. These cannot be deducted during the tax year they are effected but added to the value of the asset (land, building or plant). Once added to the capital cost of the property and its components (furniture and equipment) capital expenditures are depreciated at their respective rates. They will also be added to the asset base and thus reduce the capital gain tax liability. For long term investors development 'soft costs' (interim financing, professional fees, mortgage fees, insurance premium, advertising and leasing expenses, etc.) are deemed capital expenditures and therefore capitalised; they are amortised over the holding period and added to the asset base used in calculating the capital gains. These costs would be treated as recurrent expenses for those whose business is developing for profit on resale.

• When expenditures are carried out on a property in need of extensive repairs and replacements at the time of acquisition, they will be treated as capital in nature even though, in other circumstances, they would be treated as current expenses.

This distinction between types of expenses leads us to a new twist in the tree presented in Chapter II. As depicted in Figure V.1, some expenditures which are deducted to determine net operating income, are not allowable operating expenses for tax purposes. Capital expenditures, consistent with our general model, should be added to the value of the asset either as additional equity when the new capital outlay is paid cash or added to the debt if financing is required.

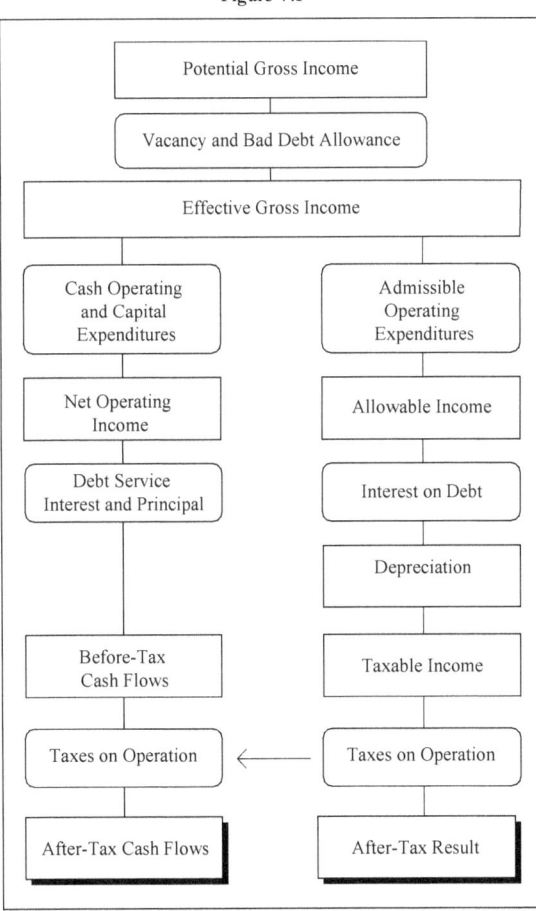

Figure V.1

1.2 The treatment of financing charges

• Only the interest portion of the debt service is deductible during the taxation year. Interest charged on all forms of debt financing (mortgage, personal loans, revolving credit, etc.) are deductible so long as such debt was contracted to generate an investment profit.

• Even mortgage interest on a loan secured on an owner occupied residence becomes deductible if the money is used to 'earn assessable income'. Otherwise, interest on owner-occupied residences is not deductible in Australia, in Singapore or in Hong Kong (in contrast with the US treatment). As we saw earlier, interim and construction financing charges cannot be deducted: they must be capitalised (added to the capital value of the asset).

• Interest paid to purchase undeveloped land are not deductible in the current year unless the property is used to generate an assessable income (*e.g.*, a parking lot). A recent judgment (the Steele case) has apparently reversed this restriction.

• Interest on a refinanced loan may not be entirely deductible if the value of the loan is greater than the market value of the asset or if the loan is not used to increase the assessable income from the property.

• The costs of establishing a loan (lender's establishment fees, legal and valuation fees, mortgage documents stamp duties and any other charges) can be deducted over the first five years of the loan or over the term of any shorter loans.

Again the principle of causal relationship must be kept in mind in order to justify the deductibility of financing charges and related expenses. The nature and amount of the debt must always be in direct relationship with the nature, value and usage of the property.[1]

• If financing charges are greater than the net taxable income from a property (or portfolio of properties), the excess can be deducted from the taxpayer's other income. This possibility of creating a 'deductible interest loss' is what is commonly referred as **'negative gearing'**. This specific problem will be discussed more fully when we are able to draw a complete picture of the various tax consequences of this apparent tax advantage.

1.3 The treatment of depreciation

• Accounting depreciation is an approximate measure of an asset's decreasing usefulness through time. Assets are depreciated until either they no longer earn income or until they are sold. This depreciation may amount to a fixed proportion of the asset's value and spread over its full economic life (linear deprecia-

---

1. Lease financing may be used to maximise the tax advantages of rental deductibility. The full amount of the rent is deductible on the full value of the property of a leasehold whereas only the interests on the levered value is deductible on a loan covering the same property. Various schemes and counter schemes are constantly being devised to structure lease arrangements that are acceptable to the Department of Taxation.

tion) or could model a more realistic decreasing drop in value (declining balance). The depreciation appears as an expense in the profit and loss statement. The written down value (the undepreciated value) of the asset appears on the asset side of the balance sheet.

• Beyond these accounting principles and practices, particular rules apply to the tax treatment of depreciation.[1] These general rules are covered in Division 40 and 41 of the ATA 1997 where the concept of 'depreciation' is more generally defined as Capital Allowances. Under the new (July 2001) Uniform Capital Allowance (UCC) system the jargon has been modified (again) and the preferred expression is now 'decline in value'.

— The deductions on buildings and structures (capital works) are limited to assets put in place after 1979. Technically capital works are not 'depreciated' but entitled to a fixed cost annual deduction calculated on the initial construction costs.

— Annual depreciation can be claimed on plant, machinery, fixtures and equipment placed in or part of a property.[2] This depreciation is deducted to compensate for the decreasing value of the assets over the years of usage. Part of this depreciation may be recaptured at disposal if the market value of the depreciated assets is greater than the undepreciated amount.

— No depreciation may be deducted on the land component of a property.

Thus for depreciation purposes, the building and the other depreciable components of a property are treated differently.

1. The treatment of capital works

Capital works are buildings, extensions, alterations or improvements to a building. It also includes related works such as roads, driveways, fences, bridges or pipelines. Such capital works may be entitled to deductions at a constant rate calculated on the initial construction cost.

The eligible construction costs are:

- construction hard costs for the buildings and its base (excavations, foundations, piling, etc.);
- construction soft costs: fees for professional services (architects, surveying, engineering, legal, etc.).

The following elements are ineligible:

---

1. Depreciation is deductible on any property owned or 'quasi-owned' by an assessable income producing tax payer. A 'quasi-owner' is a lessee of a leased Crown Land.
2. The concept of plant is very general. It may include any machinery, tools, rolling stock, fences, dams, structural improvements, plumbing fittings, even animals used as carriers in a business. Depreciation may also be taken by a lessee of assets affixed to land under a Crown lease.

- land costs (hard and soft), site preparation and landscaping;
- demolition of existing structure.

The choice of deduction rate depends on the intended destination, the nature and the date of construction of the property. The legislation has evolved constantly since 1979 and the most recent rules were adopted in 2001. In general, constructions put after 1979 may apply a 2.5% or 4% rate to the cost of construction[1] depending on the nature of the building, the intended usage and the date of construction. This allowance continues for 40 (for a rate of 2.5%) or 25 years (for a rate of 4%) from first use of the building.

For buildings acquired after May 1997, the deduction entitlement is deducted from the asset base in order to compute capital gains tax (there was no recapture before 1997). For building acquired after July 2001, we are now down to a depreciation of **2.5%** per year.

The treatment of capital works and depreciations is another zone of the Australian Tax Act that is remarkably inept, inequitable and which begs for a drastic rewriting.

2. The treatment of plants (now defined as 'depreciable assets')

For tax calculations, items of plant or machinery within a building (such as lifts, air-conditioning systems, carpets, curtains, kitchen fittings and other equipment) may be depreciated using either the straight line or declining balance method[2] (Since February 1992[3]). Depreciable assets may be treated item per item or pooled together for items with the same depreciation rates and usage.

Plants that cost 300 $ or less or which have an effective life shorter than three years are deductible at 100% of their purchase value in the year of acquisition. This immediate deduction applies only to goods acquired after 1 July 1991.

For each specific asset, the taxpayer may apply indicative rates suggested by the Tax Office: the 'safe harbour rate' (Income Tax ruling IT 2685) to the declining balance of the assets (Column 2 in table V.3). He may also choose to apply the straight line method also using the suggested rates (Column 3 in table V.3). Once a rate and method has been chosen for a depreciable item, the same conditions must be applied in successive years.

Depreciation deductions are pro-rated for the number of days in the year from the construction date or the put-in-use date.

---

1. Construction costs include design fees and excavation but exclude site costs and plant.
2. The straight line method is also referred as 'prime cost' method. And the declining balance is referred as 'diminishing value' method.
3. Assets owned prior 27 February 1992 are also depreciable according to the same schedules but the rates have been different at different periods.

Very generally the following rates would apply depending on the date of construction and the intended usage of the building. Check your IPA website for updating, computations and examples.

Table V.2   Depreciation rates applicable to the plant, machinery and equipment components of a property

1 Depreciable assets (examples)	2 Annual rate applied to declining balance (Diminishing value rates)	3 Annual rate applied to straight line depreciation (Prime cost rates)
Blind	8%	5%
Carpets	15%	10%
Refrigerators	11%	8%
Washing machines	23%	15%
Lawn mower	30%	20%

A 100% rate also applies to plant costing 300 $ or less. Cars, motorcycles and artwork have different depreciation rates. Assets of similar effective lives can be pooled in a single group in order to simplify the depreciation calculations.

If a property is sold again, the plant can be depreciated from the undeducted cost that the vendor has reached or from the declared contractual value for the plant certified by an expert. Thus this treatment is more flexible than the one applied to building deduction where the buyer has no choice but to take the undeducted cost left over from the vendor.

Example of depreciation and deduction schedules

Acquisition: August 2003	
Cost of the building	100,000$
Contractual value of the fixtures and equipment	7,000$
- Lawn mowers (straight line method also called prime cost method)	20%
- Carpets (diminishing value method)	15%

Table V.3 Depreciation schedule over the first five years[1]

Years	Deduction on building	Adjustable value	Fixture and equipment (lawn mowers)	Adjustable value	Fixture and equipment (carpets)	Adjustable value
	2.5% on building cost		Annual rate of 20% until full depreciation		Annual rate of 15% on diminishing balance	
0		100,000		2,000		5,000
1	2,500	97,500	400	1,600	750	4,250
2	2,500	95,000	400	1,200	638	3,613
3	2,500	92,500	400	800	542	3,071
4	2,500	90,000	400	400	461	2,610
5	2,500	87,500	400	0	392	2,219

1.4 The treatment of operating losses

A real operating loss may occur when operating expenditures in a year are larger than operating revenues. Furthermore a 'tax loss' may also occur if deductible financing charges and depreciations are greater that the assessable income from the property (or portfolio of properties).

These tax losses can be deducted from other incomes during the tax year or carried forward to the next fiscal year. Such losses will reduce the amount of taxes payable, may reduce the marginal rates or, if they are large enough, may eliminate all taxable incomes. Unused tax losses can always be carried forward against future income.[2] Strangely enough the losses cannot be carried backward.

2. Taxation at disposal

At least two tax consequences must be considered upon disposal of a property: 1) part of the depreciation claimed during the holding period may be recaptured and 2) capital gains may be taxed.

But before we get down to the details of this terminal treatment, we should first point out that there are many different ways to 'dispose' of a property and not all of these give rise to tax immediately (Table V.5). In fact we now have more than fifty possible capital gain taxable events (CGT events) however, we could limit the property related examples to the following events.

---

1. During the years of purchase and disposal, these tax deductions are apportioned according to the number of days that the taxpayer owned the property during the tax year (which starts on 1 July in Australia). For our purpose of financial analysis, it is normal to assume full year deductions until fully claimed, even if the property is not being acquired at the start of a tax year.

2. Pre-July 89 losses can be carried forward to a maximum of 7 years. Then losses can be carried forward indefinitely.

Table V.4 Disposal: immediate or deferred taxation

Transactions that trigger taxation in the year of disposal
- Sale
- Exchange of assets
- Gift (treated as disposal at market value)
- Foreclosure
- Demolition or destruction
- Transfer to a trust or estate
- Sale of shares or other interest of entity owning properties
- Ceasing residency in Australia

Transactions that may defer taxation
- Compulsory acquisition provided a replacement property is acquired
- Insurance compensation provided a replacement property is acquired
- Inheritance
- Some business reorganisation that do not change the beneficial ownership

2.1 The taxation of capital gains

In Australia, capital gains are taxed when the disposal price of a property is greater than its net acquisition cost for property acquired or built after 20 September 1985 (properties acquired before this date are not submitted to this tax treatment). Capital losses occur in the opposite situation (nevertheless capital losses cannot occur on the sale of depreciable assets since any loss would be treated as a terminal depreciation).

Capital gains are added to the taxpayer's assessable income and thus taxed at the marginal tax rate. But the treatment is not symmetrical since capital losses cannot be deducted from assessable income, they can only be deducted against capital gains in the year of taxation or any future year (carried forward).

Capital gains may apply to a great variety of the assets (collectables, personal use goods, shares, goodwill etc.) and, in our domain, they will also apply to transactions on unit trusts (ex: Listed Property Trusts), on leases and on rights and options.[1]

---

1. Properties bought and resold within 12 months are subjected to a capital gain without inflation indexation of the acquisition costs or without the benefit of the discount method (see below). Similarly, transactions on properties by taxpayers whose main activity is to deal in properties and developments will be treated as normal profits. A prorated capital gain will apply to a residence leased for a portion of a time of ownership.

Generally speaking, capital gains arising from transactions on owner-occupied residences are tax exempt[1] as long as the residence is not used to produce income.

Table V.5   Capital gains taxation: jargon and mechanic

1- Proceeds of disposal	Gross sale price or market value of the compensation received minus the costs of disposal (brokerage fees, professional fees, loan prepayments, etc.).
2- Cost base	Purchase price + incidental expenses of acquisition[2] + initial and interim capital expenditures incurred to increase the value of the asset + initial and interim non capital expenditure for assets acquired after 20/8/91.[3]
	Inflation adjustment of the cost base is now (after 2001) optional and nowadays less favourable than the discount method
3- Reduced cost base	Cost base minus accumulated decline in value
4- Taxable capital gain	The difference between proceeds of disposal and the reduced asset base: 4 = 1 - 3.
	Capital losses can only be offset against capital gains.
5- Capital gain tax	Under the discount method, half of the capital gain is assessable. (only for individuals and Trusts). For complying superannuation funds 2/3 of the capital gains are assessable and 100% of the capital gains are assessable if the assets have been held less than one year.

---

1. Including up to 2 hectares of land. The principal residence exemption can be maintained up to 6 years (renewable) if the property is rented 'temporarily'. But the exemption is reduced if the property is partly used to produce income. The reduction will be pro-rated to the level of 'non residential' usage of the house.
2. Soft service costs: accounting, surveying, valuing, legal advises, consulting, duties and stamps, advertising, etc.
3. Interest on money borrowed to acquire or improve the asset, maintaining, repairing and insuring the asset, rates or land taxes. Strangely enough, these non-capital costs cannot be indexed whereas the other components of the cost base can be indexed.

Table V.6 The Quintus building submitted to capital gain

1.	Gross acquisition price	120,000 $
2.	Acquisition costs (legal fees, agent commissions, etc.)	6,000 $
3.	Further capital enhancement expenditures	0 $
4.	Asset Cost Base = 1 + 2 + 3	126,000 $
5.	Capital allowance deducted during holding period	12,000 $
6.	Adjusted asset base = 4 - 5	114,000 $
8.	Disposal	200,000 $
9.	Disposal costs	10,000 $
10.	Capital gain = 8 - 9 - 6	76,000 $
11.	Taxable capital gain (discount method) = (8 - 9 - 6)/2	**38,000 $**
12	Other taxable income (from other sources)	30,000 $
13.	Tax payable without capital gain	5,682 $
14.	Total taxable income	68,000 $
15.	Total tax payable	**19 923 $**
Thus the taxation of capital gain increases the tax amount by		14,241 $
Thus in this case the effective taxation % of capital gain is		37.48%

2.2 Recapture on depreciable assets

The recapture (claw-back) of excess plant depreciation is part of the assessment of income tax during the year of disposal. Disposing of a property may result in recapture of some of the depreciation allowance if the plant is sold for more than its depreciated value (too much depreciation was taken).

When plant is sold for more than its undepreciated value, the excess is added to the taxpayer's income in that year (unless a substitute item of plant is acquired). The recapture of excess plant depreciation, which is known as a balancing adjustment, is added to the taxable income in the year of sale.

Conversely, if the termination value was less than the undeducted cost, a deductible balancing adjustment would be allowed. (Not enough depreciation has been taken...) In this situation, the balancing adjustment will be deductible from the taxable income.

Although the balancing adjustment arises only on disposal of the property, it should not be confused with the computation of the capital gains tax. They must be treated quite separately in the final disposal computation.

The computation of the balancing charge can be illustrated with the following graphs.

Where: WDV = Written down value. Now called 'adjustable value'

NAC = Net acquisition cost

TV = Termination value

1. The termination value is below the written down value (not enough depreciation was taken). The balancing adjustment is deductible from the taxpayer income.

```
        TV        WDV                      NAC
        |          |      Depreciation      |
────────┼──────────┼───────────────────────┼────────
        |Deductible|                        |
```

2. The termination value is greater than the written down value but smaller than the amount of depreciation taken off. In this case the balancing adjustment is equal to the difference between TV and WDV and added to the taxpayer assessable income. Alternatively the taxpayer may deduct this recapture from the initial value of a replacement asset. This option, also called offset option, has the advantage of delaying the assessment of the depreciation recapture. In this case the deduction must be taken in priority from the value of the replacement asset, then eventually the value of any other assets acquired in the same year, and finally the deduction may be taken against the written down value of other existing assets.

```
                WDV        TV              NAC
                 |■ ■ ■ ■ ■|                |
─────────────────┼─────────┼────────────────┼──────
                 | Recaptured               |
```

3. The termination value is above the original costs. In this case, the full depreciation taken will be recaptured. But the excess amount will not be assessable under the same conditions: it will be treated as ordinary business income and eventually subjected to capital gain.

```
                WDV                NAC      TV
                 |■ ■ ■ ■ ■ ■ ■ ■ ■|        |
─────────────────┼─────────────────┼────────┼──────
                 |   Recaptured    |
```

Under the offset provisions of section 42-285, the reader can conclude that the claw-back mechanism has very few... teeth, since the recapture can be postponed as long as the taxpayer has some depreciable assets in his portfolio.

2.3 Rozy meets the tax person

We will now provide the full operating example of the Rozy building introduced in Chapter II. The complete financial and fiscal analysis will be presented in Chapter VII, but now we can illustrate how to apply the main fiscal rules:

deductions for loan interest and establishment charges, building deduction and plant depreciation, taxation of capital gains and recapture.

In this very simplified case, the depreciable assets are sold at their adjustable value (thus no recapture) and we do not assume any additional capital expenditures or improvements. More interesting and complex cases should be practiced in the spreadsheets provided in the IPA website.

Table V.7 Rozy's capital allowance and depreciation schedules

Depreciation schedules			
Building:	70 000 $	Rate: 2.5 %	
Depreciable asset	10 000 $	Rate: 30 %	Diminishing value method
Years of operation:	5		
Capital allowance on the building			
Initial cost	Years	Capital allowance	Adjustable value
70 000 $	1	1,750 $	68,250 $
	2	1,750 $	66,500 $
	3	1,750 $	64,750 $
	4	1,750 $	63,000 $
	5	1,750 $	61,250 $
Total allowance		8,750 $	
Decline in value of depreciable asset (at 30% declining value)			
Initial Value	Year	Decline in value	Adjustable value
10,000.00 $	1	3,000.00 $	7,000.00 $
	2	2,100.00 $	4,900.00 $
	3	1,470.00 $	3,430.00 $
	4	1,029.00 $	2,401.00 $
	5	720.30 $	1,680.70 $
Total decline in value		8,319.30 $	

Table V.8 Computation of the net income and cash flow at disposal

	FISCAL CONSEQUENCES OF DISPOSAL		
	Gross disposal price	Transaction costs	Net disposal price
Building	80,000 $	3,200 $	76,800 $
Land	39,257 $	1,570 $	37,687 $
Depreciable assets	1,751 $	70 $	1,681 $
Total	121,008 $	4,840 $	116 168 $
Balancing adjustments			0 $
Total net disposal price			116 168 $
Net disposal price (Land and building)			114,488 $
Less: prepayment penalty			608 $
Net proceeds			113,880 $
Asset base			90,000 $
Less: building allowance			8,750 $
Reduced asset base			81,250 $
Capital gain			32,630 $
Taxable capital gain (discount method)			16,315 $
Marginal rate			48.7%
Taxation on capital gain			**7,945 $**
Taxation on balancing adjustment			**0 $**
Taxation on disposal			**7,945 $**

CASH FLOWS AT DISPOSAL	
Gross disposal price	121,008 $
(Minus) Transaction costs	4,840 $
Net disposal price	116,168 $
(Minus) Outstanding debt	60,807 $
(Minus) Prepayment penalty	608 $
Before-tax equity reversion	54,753 $
(Minus) Taxes on disposal	7,945 $
After-tax equity residual	**46,808 $**

Chapter VI

Investment return measurement

Where we learn how to assess the performance of a real estate investment as measured over a single year (static indicators) and over the whole holding period (dynamic indicators). Where we introduce the most important formula of this book (the equity model). Some bells and whistles are presented in Appendix VI.1 and, in Appendix VI.2, we touch upon the financial leverage puzzle.

The performance of property investments must be judged on the strength of the yearly operating results and on the expectation of the resale value at the end of the holding period. This measurement can be made with the help of very simple criteria, or it can be made through more sophisticated financial models. The very simple criteria are based on the observation of a single year's performance (any year during the holding period) and are thus called static indicators (snapshot view). Other more realistic criteria are based on the actual or anticipated total performance of the asset where the evolution of incomes, expenses and the resale value are taken into account. These criteria will be labelled dynamic indicators of performance since they are computed over more than one year (movie view).

1. Static indicators

In this chapter we will introduce the most generally used tools of the real estate trade. These static 'rule of thumb' indicators are simplistic and can often be misleading. However, if understood and calculated properly, they can be very useful indeed when, as is almost always the case in this industry, 'time is of the essence'.

Depending on the chosen presentation, static indicators can be read as average rates of return (expressed in %) or as 'multipliers.' The equivalence of the two forms (rates or multiples) must remain clear in the reader's mind even though, in actual practice, each indicator is used predominantly under only one form.

Beyond these return criteria, the investor may also want to use different operating and financing static ratios which are very similar to the financial management ratios found in standard finance textbooks.

Before going further into this chapter, a warning is in order to explain the difference of precision required in the treatment of mortgage computations and the treatment of analysis of returns.

Mortgage computations must not only be accurate, but they also have to be very precise. A mortgage contract is legally binding and its terms and conditions must be adhered to very strictly. This is why we have been careful over such details as the number of decimal digits or the effects of rounding on the monthly payments and the outstanding balance. The required precision for tax computation is less severe but still the numbers should be accurate to at least the nearest dollar.

On the other hand, investment analysis is a predictive exercise. The value of a property and of its annual returns are estimated on the basis of anticipated cash flows, on hypotheses concerning mortgage rates, the strength of the market, the occupancy level, the inflation rate, the dynamism of the competitors, the life expectancy of the janitor and, of course, the value of the Japanese Yen!

These forecasts are inescapably fairly fuzzy and only the foolish analyst would put too much faith in his capacity to anticipate all the numbers precisely. In any predictive financial analysis, you have to accept that corners must be cut, that numbers will not square off and that most of your results will be, at best, very vaguely 'right.' Accordingly the following general simplifications will be adopted:

— Revenues and expenses will be considered as if they were received or expended at the end of the year. Thus monthly rental payments (made at the beginning of each month), bimonthly water charges and annual insurance payments will all be lumped together at the end of the year.

— The initial equity is assumed to be invested at the beginning of the first year. All subsequent capital expenditures, whenever they occur, will be discounted back to the beginning of the first year and added to the initial equity investment.

— Compounding and discounting computations are treated as simple annuities on a yearly basis and thus the relevant rate will always be the nominal rate. Of course this does not apply to the computation of the mortgage factors (payments and outstanding balance).

— The dollar results can be rounded to the closest 100 dollars for annual flows and to the closest 1,000 dollars for values.

1.1 Static indicators of performance

The main static indicators are presented at Table VI.1 in the order of the different computational stages discussed in Chapter II (from the potential gross income to the after-tax cash flows). Each indicator is shown under its two reciprocal guises: as a rate of return and as a multiplier.

Table VI.1   Static performance criteria

		Rate of return	Multipliers	Comments
Gross Income	GI	GI/V	V/GI	Commonly used as a multiple. The gross income multiplier GIM can be computed on the potential gross income or, preferably, on effective gross income.
Net Operating Income	NOI	NOI/V	V/NOI	Used as a rate of return on the net (the valuers' capitalisation rate) or as a net income multiplier: NIM.
Before-Tax Cash Flow	BTCF	BTCF/E_0	E_0/BTCF	A 'cash on cash' rate and also the valuers' dividend rate (**y**) to meet in chapter X.
After-Tax Cash Flow	ATCF	ATCF/E_0	E_0/ATCF	These rates and multipliers are not commonly used since they require a more complex analysis of the tax situation.
Notation:	V	Value of the property		
	GI	Gross Income		
	E_0	Initial equity investment (in year 0)		
	NOI	Net operating income		
	BTCF	Before-tax cash flow = NOI - PMT		
	ATCF	After-tax cash flow = NOI - PMT - Taxes on operation		

We will now review and illustrate each individual criterion with the help of a very simple example: the Sextus Building (Rozy will come back in due time, don't fret).

Table VI.2   The Sextus building

Asking price (V)	48,000$
Mortgage (D)	38,000$
Nominal rate ($i_{12,12}$) on 120 months	8%
Effective gross income	8,000$
Operating expenses	2,000$
Anticipated income tax (on operating revenues)	600$

1.1.1   Gross income criteria

• The Gross Income Multiplier

This is probably the best (but not the brightest) of the *quick and dirty* criteria. It is expressed as the ratio of a value (purchase price, asking price, assessed value) and a gross income. The required gross income could be the potential or (better) the effective gross income. Valuers may also have to use a 'normalised' gross income. This is an adjusted value of the stated gross income which would reflect the normal long term operating conditions of the property (see Chapter IX).

The Gross Income Multiplier is written:

GIM = Value/Gross Income

GIM = V/GI

The GIM for our Sextus investment would thus be:

GIM = 48,000$/8,000$ = 6

In traditional analysis, this multiplier is usually presented as a pay back period. That is the number of years required to recover the total purchase price of the asset. In this example, a GIM of 6 implies that it takes 6 years of gross income to recover the 48,000$ full value of the property.

• The Gross Rate of Return

Under its reciprocal form, the GIM turns into a Gross Rate of Return (GRR):

GRR = Gross Income/Value

GRR = GI/V

Thus, for Sextus:

GRR = 8,000$/48,000$ = 16.66%

The inverse relationship between rates and multipliers is illustrated as follows:

Gross Income Multiplier	GIM	4	5	6	7	8
Gross Rate of Return	GRR	25%	20%	16.6%	14.2%	12.5%

Thus a GIM of 5 implies a 20% gross return on the total value of the investment. You may think that you are doing quite well if you pay 5 times its annual gross income for a property since it means that you obtain 20% on your money. It's better than a booming ASX return! But is it really?

Of course it is not since this 20% rate is a gross rate. This gross rate is the rate of return before operating expenses, before debt repayment and before taxes. To use the GRR as a useful comparison you should match it with returns on alternative similar investments. Here 'similar' means that those other investments should have the same relative share of operating expenses, the same amount of debt and the same taxation status. Since very few financial instruments (stocks, bonds, options, treasury bills, rare stamps, etc.) are likely to fit this description, the comparison will likely be invalid. Indeed the GRR on real properties can only be compared with the GRR on similar real properties and not with alternative financial vehicles.

Thus, if the Sextus gross income is 8,000$, the appraised value could be 48,000$ if the GIM observed on recent market transactions is 6.

The GIM should be used carefully and with a proper knowledge of market conditions and operating characteristics of different types of properties. This risk is particularly serious because, as we have seen in Chapter I, the real estate market is so fragmented that it could be more appropriately described as a patchwork of interrelated sub-markets[1]. To put numbers on this diversity, we can observe that the 'typical' Australian GIM for residential income properties ranges between 4 and 10 depending on the size of the building, its age, its location and its appropriate State rental legislation.

1.1.2 Net operating income criteria

We have just realized that the Gross Income Multiplier does not take the operating characteristics of a property directly into account and we may feel more comfortable with an 'after-expenses' type of criteria. This indicator is computed on the Net Operating Income, *i.e.,* net of operating expenses but still before-debt and before-taxes.

• As a multiplier the Net Income Multiplier is now:

NIM   =   V/NOI

In the 'UK-sphere' this rate is usually called a 'years purchase' rate.

•As a rate of operating return, the reciprocal of the NIM is the Net Rate of Return (NRR) which may also be labelled a 'brokers' net' or, less appropriately, a 'free and clear rate of return' or also, by the valuers, the 'overall capitalisation rate' (the cap. rate of Chapter IX):

NRR   =   NOI/V

For Sextus, the multipliers and rates would thus be:

GI   =   8,000$
NOI   =   6,000$
V   =   48,000$
NIM   =   48,000$/6,000$
      =   8
NRR   =   6,000$/48,000$
      =   12.5%

The relationship between the Gross Income Multiplier, the operating efficiency (ratio ß = NOI/GI to be discussed further below) and the Net Income Multiplier can be illustrated below:

---

1. See Appendix VI.1 for an extension to valuing adjustments and for the transition from GIM to Net income multiplier.

INCOME PROPERTY ANALYSIS

Table VI.3 GIM, NIM and ß = NOI/GI

	GIM	3.0	4.0	5.0	6.0	7.0	8.0
NOI/GI = 0.60	NIM	5.0	6.6	8.3	10.0	11.6	13.3
NOI/GI = 0.50	NIM	6.0	8.0	10.0	12.0	14.0	16.0
NOI/GI = 0.40	NIM	7.5	10.0	12.5	15.0	17.5	20.0

As we did with the GIM, let us insist once more on the reciprocal nature of a multiplier (pay back period) and its corresponding rate of return.

Net Income Multiplier	NIM	5	8	10	12	14
Net Rate of Return	NRR	20%	12.5%	10%	8.3%	7.1%

Thus a purchase price of 8 times the Net Operating Income implies a 12.5% after-expenses, before-debt and before-tax rate of return. Now this type of return could more appropriately be compared to the returns on other financial instruments (stocks, bonds, etc.) but this comparison would still be quite fragile since the respective levels of risk are different for such investments and, most importantly, because these NIM-NRR indicators are static criteria. They do not take the resale value into account.

1.1.3 Cash flow criteria

Since debt is such an important part of property investment, the investor should be mostly concerned with the after-debt returns. In a static format, the only common cash return measurement is computed on the before-tax cash flows.

Here again we may use the two reciprocal forms:

— The before-tax equity return (also called the cash-on-cash return or the equity dividend rate). In this formula E_0 is the initial equity investment at time 0:

$$BTER = BTCF/E_0$$
$$BTER = (NOI - PMT)/E_0$$

— A rarely used cash flow multiplier (or cash pay back period) form can also be written:

$$CFM = E_0/BTCF$$

Back to Sextus to illustrate our new BTER and CFM criteria.

Table VI.4 Cash returns on Sextus

Mortgage (D)	38,000$
Nominal rate	8%
n	180 months
NOI	6,000$
Initial equity	10,000$

We write:

$$\text{BTER} = \frac{\text{Annual Net Operating Income} - \text{Annual Debt Service}}{\text{Equity Investment}}$$

$$= (6,000\$ - 4,358\$)/10,000\$$$

BTER = 16.4%

And expressed as the cash flow multiplier:

CFM = 1/BTER
= 1/0.164
= 6.09

In pay back period terms, this result means that the invested equity of 10,000$ can be recovered from the before-tax cash proceeds in 6 years.

Quite clearly this cash-on-cash return depends directly on the amount of equity invested. In Sextus, the cash return increases when the invested cash decreases: this is the typical (and misleading illustration) of a favourable financial leverage effect (see Appendix VI.2). Of course, the cash return is equal to the net income return in the absence of financing. Table VI.5 illustrates these relationships with the Sextus example.

Table VI.5 Debt and cash returns for Sextus

Equity investment ($)	5,000	10,000	15,000	20,000	48,000
BTER	21.38%	16.4%	14.77%	13.95%	12.50%
CFM	4.68	6.09	6.77	7.17	8

The previous illustration should again be used as a warning against the occasional misrepresentation of those criteria by vendors who may quote juicy returns without specifying the required assumptions. (For some more examples of misrepresentation see Appendix VI.1).

1.2   Operating and financial indicators of performance

Further criteria can be used to judge the management and financing characteristics of a property. These operating and financial ratios are also commonly used in ordinary management finance or accounting and thus they will be very briefly described in Table VI.6.

Table VI.6 Static operating and financial ratios

Liquidity ratios		
Debt to Value Ratio (Debt/Value)	D/V	This ratio is an important measure of the financial risk borne by the investor.
Debt Coverage Ratio (Net operating income/annual mortgage payment)	NOI/PMT	Measures the extent to which net operating income can cover the mortgage payment.
Financial Margin	$\dfrac{\text{NOI} - \text{PMT}}{\text{NOI}}$	Another form of the previous indicator.
Profitability ratios		
Operating Expenses Ratio (Operating Expenses/Gross Income)	OE/GI	An indicator of management efficiency also presented in a complementary form (NOI/GI = 1 - OE/GI).
Break Even Ratio	$\dfrac{\text{OE} + \text{PMT}}{\text{GI}}$	This ratio gives the minimal occupancy rate for which expenses are covered by gross income.
Profit Margin Ratio	BTCF/GI	A complementary form of the previous ratio and measures the operating residual.

1.2.1 Liquidity ratios

These ratios are used by investors and, even more importantly, by lenders to assess the financial soundness of an investment or a loan. They are good proxies of the financial risk involved in the investment.

• The Debt to Value ratio is a direct measurement of the relative share of debt outstanding to the value of the property.

D/V = Debt/Value

This ratio is used extensively in property analysis, in mortgage finance and also in corporate finance to adjust the discount rate (see Appendix VI.2). Of course, the D/V ratio will not be constant over the holding period. It will decrease through the amortisation of the loan and it will increase with the refinancing of the property. Accordingly the financial risk borne by the investor will decrease (amortisation) or increase (refinancing).

An equivalent ratio can also be used as a complement to the D/V:

E/V = Equity/Value
E/V = (1- D/V)

Or:

E/D = Equity/Debt
E/D = E/(V-E)

For Sextus, the resulting ratios would be:

D/V = 38,000$/48,000$
    = 79.1%

E/V = 10,000\$/48,000\$
 = 20.8%
E/D = 10,000\$/38,000\$
 = 26.3%

• The Debt Coverage Ratio[1] measures the extent to which the NOI will cover the annual payments.

$DCR = NOI/PMT$

$$DCR = \frac{\text{Net Operating Income}}{\text{Annual Debt Service}}$$

This ratio has to be greater than 1 and typically lenders will require a minimum ratio of 1.25 (leaving a security 'cushion' of 25%). Higher ratios will be required on riskier types of investment properties (industrial building, hotels, motels, etc.).

1.2.2 Operating ratios

• The ratio of operating expenses to the gross income (OE/GI) is the simplest indicator of management efficiency among similar properties.

$$\frac{OE}{GI} = \frac{\text{Operating Expenses}}{\text{Gross Income}}$$

Its complement, NOI/GI (or 1 - OE/GI), has been used previously in this chapter to adjust the Gross Income Multiplier.

$$\frac{NOI}{GI} = \frac{\text{Net Operating Income}}{\text{Gross Income}}$$

These ratios (OE/GI or NOI/GI) ought to be used only to compare properties which have similar operating characteristics. Comparing different types of properties or properties located in different areas may lead to poor investment decisions. Comparisons would be even more misleading between residential properties and shopping centres or office buildings in which most of the operating charges are (increasingly) supported by the tenants and not by the owner.

• The break even ratio is expressed as a percentage of minimum occupancy required to 'break even' *i.e.*, in this context, to cover the operating and financing charges. This ratio can be measured as a percentage of rooms occupied in a hotel, suites rented in an apartment building, square footage in an office building or shopping centre. This important indicator will be taken up again in Chapter VIII:

$$BE = \frac{OE + PMT}{GI}$$

---

1. See Appendix VI.1 for the link between the DCR and the Security Margin Ratio.

- The profit margin (BTCF/GI = Before-Tax Cash Flow/Gross Income) is the complement of the break even ratio. It is the net residual left after operating and financing expenses have been met:

$$PM = \frac{GI - OE - PMT}{GI} = \frac{BTCF}{GI}$$

Our brand new tools can now be tested on Sextus (Table VI.7).

Table VI.7 Operating Rratios of the Sextus building

Expense Ratio	$\frac{OE}{GI}$	=	$\frac{2,000\$}{8,000\$}$	=	25%
Net to Gross Ratio	$\frac{NOI}{GI}$	=	$\frac{6,000\$}{8,000\$}$	=	75%
Break Even	$\frac{OE + PMT}{GI}$	=	$\frac{2,000\$ + 4,358\$}{8,000\$}$	=	79.5%
Profit Margin	$\frac{BTCF}{GI}$	=	$\frac{1,642\$}{8,000\$}$	=	20.5%

2. Dynamic return measurements

2.1 The general equity model

The previous indicators were defined as static since they are based on a single year analysis of the property's performance. They could be compared to a snapshot taken at some specific time (usually at the start) of the holding period. Even when these static indicators are used in a dynamic fashion by tracing static indicators from one year to the next during the entire holding period (*i.e.*, pasting a whole set of snapshots), they still cannot provide the full picture of the investment; they cannot appropriately include the full taxation and disposition consequences of the property.

This difference is paramount to the property investor. She needs to know the end of the story and thus she must incorporate the full consequences of the disposition of her property in the analysis.

A very simple analogy could be useful to clarify this distinction between a static and dynamic indicator. A share is bought for 100$ at the beginning of the year and yields a 5$ dividend by the end of the first year. The 'static' rate of return would be 5%. If the share is sold for 110$ at the end of the year, the 'dynamic'[1] return is now 15%.

---

1. In this one period example the meaning of the word 'dynamic' is stretched a bit since normally it would take more that a year to qualify as a dynamic criterion and indeed such measurements are performed on the entire holding period which is normally longer that a year.

Our objective is now to introduce the two most important dynamic criteria which will encapsulate the results of the entire investment cycle from the initial equity investment to the operation, taxation and disposition of the property. These indicators are the very common workhorses of traditional corporate finance: the Net Present Value and the Internal Rate of Return.

Here, in real estate analysis, we diverge from the traditional corporate finance treatment since we deal with **equity** investment and **equity** return. Thus we will set up an **after-financing** formulation of the present value and internal rate of return. These words have to be set in bold characters because this distinction is crucial and not always well understood. Property models are computed after-debt whereas traditional corporate finance models are computed before-debt.

The most general depiction of the equity model is given in Figure VI.1.

Figure VI.1

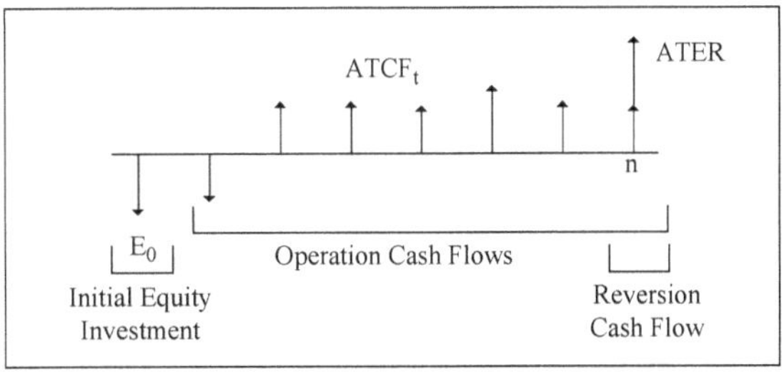

[Diagram: timeline showing E_0 (Initial Equity Investment) at start, $ATCF_t$ as Operation Cash Flows over periods, and $ATER$ (Reversion Cash Flow) at year n]

In Greek, the net present value of this investment will be noted:

$$NPV = \sum_{t=1}^{t=n} \frac{ATCF_t}{(1+k_e)^t} + \frac{ATER_n}{(1+k_e)^n} - E_0$$

| Summation of present values of the After-Tax Cash Flows for each **t** year of the holding period | Present value of After-Tax Equity Reversion in year **n** | Initial Equity investment |

This is probably the most important formula in the book.

If the reader wishes to memorize a single piece of information, this should be the one, keeping in mind the following crucial proviso:

> k_e the discount rate used in this equity model should be the rate expected by the investor after-debt and after-tax. This rate must thus take into account the fiscal situation (measured by the effective rate of taxation) and the financing load (measured by the ratio D/E) borne by the property.

2.2 The Net Present Value

The concept of net present value has already been introduced in Chapter III and we will now illustrate its detailed calculation with a Sextus-II simplistic example (Tables VI.8 and VI.9) where the after-tax cash flows will be discounted at the after-debt and after-tax expected equity rate of return k_e (net-net equity rate) of 10%.

Table VI.8 The financial story of Sextus-II (in dollars)

Initial investment at the beginning of the first year	-20,000
After-tax cash flows at the end of the first year	4,000
After-tax cash flows at the end of the second year	5,000
After-tax disposition proceeds at the end of the second year	21,000

Table VI.9 The Net Present Value calculation (in dollars)

Year	After-Tax Cash Flows	Factor (P/F, k_e, n) for $k_e = 10\%$	Present Value with $k_e = 10\%$
0	- 20,000	1.00	- 20,000
1	4,000	0.91	3,636
2	5,000	0.83	4,132
2	21,000	0.83	17,355
Net Present Value			**5,123**

Or, in the algebraic form:

$$NPV = \sum_{t=1}^{t=n} \frac{ATCF_t}{(1+k_e)^t} + \frac{ATER_n}{(1+k_e)^n} - E_0$$

$$= 7,768\$ + 17,355\$ - 20,000\$$$

$$= 5,123\$$$

Here the initial cash equity investment of 20,000$ yields 10% **and** a cash surplus of 5,123$. The investor obtains his expected minimal return of 10% and receives an extra 5,123$ to boot.

If he had invested 25,123$, his return would have been exactly 10%; but since he invested only 20,000$ his return is obviously greater that 10% and this effective greater rate of return is the Internal Rate of Return.

2.3 The Internal Rate of Return

The internal rate of return (IRR) is the discount rate for which the present value of the cash flows is equal to zero:

$$NPV = \sum_{t=1}^{t=n} \frac{ATCF_t}{(1+k_e)^t} + \frac{ATER_n}{(1+k_e)^n} - E_0 = 0$$

Here a trial and error procedure (an iterative procedure) illustrates how we will start bracketing our IRR between 10% (for which the net present value is positive) and 30% (for which the net present value is negative).

Table V.10   Sextus-II' internal rate of return: the first iterative steps

Year	ATCF (net-net)	Factors (P/F, k_e, n) for k_e = 10%	Present Values for k_e = 10%	Factors (P/F, k_e, n) for k_e = 30%	Present Values for k_e = 30%
0	- 20,000.00	1.00	- 20,000.00	1.00	- 20,000.00
1	4,000.00	0.91	3,636.36	0.77	3,076.92
2	26,000.00	0.83	21,487.60	0.59	15,384.62
Net Present Value			5,123.97		-1,538.46

This process could be continued with successive narrowing of the discount rate bracket until the net present value is equal (or close to) zero. Nowadays this painful iterative procedure is advantageously replaced by the use of the **'IRR'** function on our calculator (or, better, with the equivalent function in a spreadsheet program).

2.4   The Maximum Bidding Price (MBP)[1]

The maximum bidding price is the highest price a rational investor would bid and still obtain his expected return. In the previous example, we concluded that the investor could have invested up to 25,123$ to get his required 10%. If we add the existing mortgage liability on the property the maximum bidding price will be:

$$V \quad = \quad V_D \quad + \quad V_E$$

Total Value   =   Debt value   +   Equity value

---

1. The max. bid price is not a return measurement but simply a convenient application of the net present value criterion.

    We chose not to present some other useless indicators such as the mid-period IRR, the profitability index or the (fallacious) Financial Management Rate of Return. The Financial Management Rate of Return was introduced by Babcock, G., Findlay, C. and Messner, S. in '*FMRR and duration: implication for real estate investment analysis*', **American Real Estate and Urban Economics Association Journal**, 1974, vol. 4, n. 3, p. 49-67 and soundly criticized (for a good example: Young, M. '*FMRR: a clever hoax*', **The Appraisal Journal**, July 1979, p. 359-369.

    We also chose not to enter into the hackneyed debate on the respective merits of the Net Present Value and the Internal Rate of Return. The outcome of this debate has been made abundantly clear for the last 20 years: the NPV criterion emerges as the undisputed winner. But, despite its numerous failings (see also Appendix VIII.1), the IRR will be kept here because it is still used extensively by practitioners.

    In the UK-sphere literature one can still find quaint definitions such as Equivalent Yield and Equated yield. An **Equivalent yield** is the IRR of a constant flow of income and resale value. An **Equated yield** is the IRR of a growing flow of income and resale value. These expressions are quite confusing, usually misunderstood and certainly useless nowadays.

With an assumed mortgage of 60 000$ in our Sextus-II property the Maximum Bid Price will be:

Max. Bid Price	=	V_D	+	V_E
MBP	=	60,000$	+	25,123$
MBP	=	85,123$		

If the full purchase price is 85,123$, the investment will yield exactly 10%. Any lower purchase price will yield a higher return (and conversely). As shown in our example: a purchase price of 80,000$ (20,000$ in equity and a 60,000$ mortgage) yields 24.45%.

3. The full tool box

3.1 Static instruments

Return performance indicators

Rates	Multipliers
Gross rate of return	**Gross income multiplier**
Net rate of return	**Net income multiplier** (year purchase)
Cash on cash rate of return	Cash multiplier
Usual ratios are in bold. The other format is rarely used.	

Financial and operation most common ratios

Financial ratios	Operating ratios
Debt to value	Operating expense
Debt coverage	Break even
Financial margin	Profit margin

3.2 Dynamic indicators and instruments

Values and rates

Value	Rate
Net present value	Internal rate of return
- of the property flows - of the equity flows	- on NOI - on BTCF - on ATCF
Maximum Bid Price	

4. Practical conclusion

This chapter is probably the easiest of the whole textbook... and it is clearly the most important. It provides the fundamental measuring tools required for property analysis and valuation.

The reader is warmly invited to play extensively with the companion IPA spreadsheet examples. And play more...

As we have been covering a lot of fairly theoretical ground in the last five chapters, we need now to integrate and to apply all the tools and concepts to our old 'Rozy' building. The following chapter (Chapter VII) will be a short but critical chapter in which we will synthesize the whole analytical process. Don't skip it!

Chapter VII

How much to pay? (or to sell...)

Where Rozy is revisited with a review of the material covered in previous chapters and where, progressively, we will conduct a fully fledged discounted cash flow analysis of a property investment.

Property investment analysis relies almost exclusively on the valuation of cash returns to the equity owner. This 'equity valuation' approach is quite specific to the real estate field as traditional corporate finance does not follow this practice. Valuation models in corporate finance compare the total cost of a project to the present value of all future Net Operating Income and the tax sheltering effects of depreciation and interest charges deductibility. These are known as total cost models or, in our parlance, property models. They do not allocate the total cost (nor the total benefits) among debtholders and shareholders. This practice is based upon a sound theoretical tenet: the investment decision should not depend on the financing decision. Property valuation traditional techniques apply the same 'total cost' concept, but this simplified treatment is too limiting in the case of heavily and variably leveraged investments such as property.

For this reason, property economists prefer to separate explicitly the investment and financing decisions. In so doing, they are in effect allocating the project's revenues among its different 'partners': the equity investor (s), the lender (s) and the tax person (s). The delineation of these separate flows of incomes discounted at the appropriate rates is the main concept behind the so-called equity models or discounted cash flow models.

In this chapter, we intend to:

1. Properly define equity flows as operating and disposal cash flows.

2. Clarify how net operating incomes are divided between equity investors, lenders and the tax authorities.

3. Assess these flows separately and draw a conclusion as to the project's investment value.

Before returning to the full treatment of the Rozy example, we may want to analyse some simplified situations to illustrate further the use of dynamic indicators presented in chapter VI.

1. Simplified discounted cash flows

• *Assuming a perpetuity*

A nice little tax-exempt property is described below. The debt is non amortised (interest only) and the NOI are constant. To obtain the resale value at the end of year 5, a capitalisation rate of 10% is applied to the NOI of year 6.

Table VII.1   An example of levered perpetuity

Mortgage debt	D	750,000 $	
Mortgage rate (cost of debt)	k_d	8%	
Expected equity return	k_e	16%	
Capitalisation rate	R	10%	
Year	NOI	PMT	BTCF
1	100,000 $	60,000 $	40,000 $
2	100,000 $	60,000 $	40,000 $
3	100,000 $	60,000 $	40,000 $
4	100,000 $	60,000 $	40,000 $
5	100,000 $	60,000 $	40,000 $
Resale end of year 5	1,000,000 $	750,000 $	250,000 $
6	100,000 $		
Present value of annual flows		239,563 $	130,972 $
Present value of disposal flows		510,437 $	119,028 $
Present values	**1,000,000 $**	**750,000 $**	**250,000 $**

1. The flow of payments to the lenders can be written:

Debt = Present value of annual payment + Present value of loan balance
Debt = PMT (P/A, k_d, 5 years) + OSB_t (P/F, k_d, 5 years)
Debt = 60,000$ (P/A, 8%, 5) + 750,000$ (P/F, 8%, 5)
D = 750,000 $

Obviously, the present value of the payments is equal to the loan value since we apply a discount rate equal to the interest rate (k_d = 8%).

2. The cash flows going to the investor can be written:

Equity = Operating cash flows (P/A, k_e, 5) + Disposal cash flow (P/F, k_e, 5)
Equity = 40,000$ (P/A, 16%, 5) + 250,000$ (P/F, 16%, 5)
E = 250,000 $

3. The total property flows can now be put together:

Value	=	Value of the debt	+	Value of the equity
V	=	V_D	+	V_E
V	=	750,000 $	+	250,000 $
V	=	1,000,000 $		

In this example, an investor would be willing to pay a maximum price of 1,000,000 $ if she wants to obtain a 16% before-tax return on her equity investment of 250,000 $. At this price, the internal rate of return on her equity is equal to 16 % ($IRR_e = 16\%$).

$$\text{Max. bid price} = 1,000,000\,\$$$
$$IRR_e = 16\%$$

This is the maximum bidding price for a buyer, but of course it could also be viewed as the maximum expected price for the seller who would like to realise a return of 16% on the same past flow of income.

This point is quite often neglected: the same model can be applied to value a past stream of cash flow in order to determine a selling price or a final return after transaction.

Let us graph the very simple combination of financial flows:

Figure VII.1

DEBT — 750,000 $, 60,000 $ — PV_D = 750,000 $

EQUITY — 250,000 $, 40,000 $ — PV_E = 250,000 $

Value = 750,000 $ + 250,000 $ = 1,000,000 $

• *But life may not be a perpetuity ...*

Our new story is quite similar but now the loan of 750,000 $ is amortised over 25 years at a nominal rate of 8% (with annual payments to simplify...). Furthermore, annual operating incomes are variable. The resale value is again computed on the NOI in year 6.

Table VII.2 Valuing variable net operating incomes

Mortgage rate (cost of debt)	k_d	8%
Amortisation period in year	n	25
Resale in year	t	5
Mortgage debt	D	750,000 $
Expected equity return	k_e	16%
Capitalisation rate	R	10%

Year	NOI	PMT	BTCF
1	100,000 $	70,259 $	29,741 $
2	101,000 $	70,259 $	30,741 $
3	103,500 $	70,259 $	33,241 $
4	117,000 $	70,259 $	46,741 $
5	142,000 $	70,259 $	71,741 $
Resale end of year 5	1,420,000 $	689,814 $	730,186 $
6	142,000 $		
Present value of annual flows		280,524 $	129,752 $
Present value of disposal flow		469,476 $	347,651 $
Present values	**1,227,403 $**	**750,000 $**	**477,403 $**

We may again want to find the present value of the respective flows.

1. The lender's flows are made up of 5 payments of 70,259$ and one outstanding balance of 689,814$.

Debt   =   Present value of annual payments + Present value of the loan balance
Debt   =   PMT (P/A , k_d , 5 years)   + OSB_t (P/F , k_d , 5 years)
Debt   =   70,259$ (P/A , 8% , 5)   +   689,814$ (P/F , 8% , 5)
D   =   750 000 $

2. The investor's flows are made up of the annual variable cash flows and a disposal flow of 730,186 $ (sale value minus the outstanding mortgage balance).

$$PV = \frac{\text{Cash flow}_1}{(1+k_e)^1} + \frac{\text{Cash flow}_2}{(1+k_e)^2} + \frac{\text{Cash flow}_3}{(1+k_e)^3} + \frac{\text{Cash flow}_4}{(1+k_e)^4} + \frac{\text{Cash flow}_5}{(1+k_e)^5} + \frac{\text{Disposal Cash flow}_5}{(1+k_e)^5}$$

$$PV = \frac{29,741}{(1+0.16)^1} + \frac{30,741}{(1+0.16)^2} + \frac{33,241}{(1+0.16)^3} + \frac{46,741}{(1+0.16)^4} + \frac{71,741}{(1+0.16)^5} + \frac{730,186}{(1+0.16)^5}$$

Equity   =   129,752 $ + 347,651 $
E   =   477,403 $

Again we write the total value identity:

Value   =   Value of the debt   +   Value of the equity

V	=	V_D	+	V_E
V	=	750,000 $	+	477,403 $
V	=	1,227,403 $[1]		

Here, the investor would be willing to pay a maximum price of 1,227,403$ in order to obtain a 16% before-tax return on her cash investment of 477,403$. At this price, the before-tax internal rate of return on the equity is equal to 16% ($IRR_e = 16\%$) and the internal rate of return to the lender is obviously $k_d = 8\%$.

> Max. bid price = 1,227,403 $
> IRR_e = 16%

The before-tax internal rate of return on the equity (IRR_e) is made up of annual cash flows and the flow at disposal. Thus it is a 'dynamic' indicator of profitability. This rate of return also happens to be the only observable rate to be read from the market. This 'reading' should be obtained by a discerning observation of investors' behaviours in comparable risk, financing and taxation situations.

The graphical illustration of this model would be:

Figure VII.2

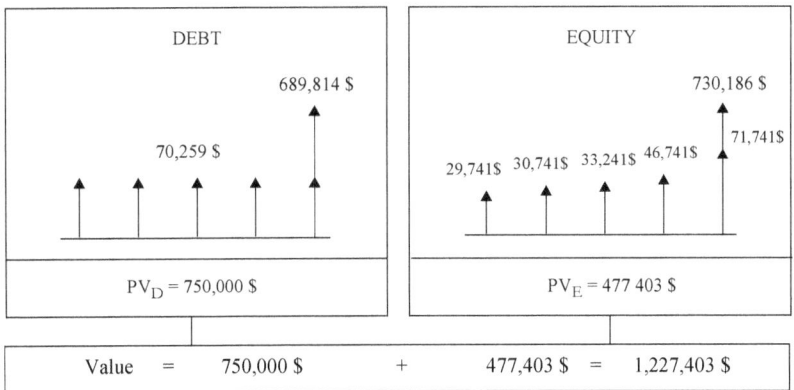

The discounting of annual cash flows is the most explicit and the most flexible of all available techniques. As we shall see next, this method can be adapted to deal with taxation and adjusted to take account of various risks (see chapter VIII).

---

1. We could not obtain the same result by a simple application of the cap. rate to the NOI. Nevertheless it is still possible to reach an approximate value by using fairly messy adjustment of the composite capitalisation rate as described in Fischer's 'Property valuation methodology', Chapter IV and appendix III.

In most countries *this approach is now considered to be the 'motherhood' technique* ... In other word, *it has become the Property Analysis paradigm.*

In Australia[1] particular care should be taken when reading and interpreting so-called DCF analysis since the expression 'Discounted Cash Flow' is confusingly used to describe the discounting of Net operating income. This practice would thus only be equivalent to the proper discounted cash flows in a simplistic 'no bank, no Queen' environment. We suggest that loose semantics lead to faulty analysis.

2. The Full Monty

The Rozy building is described again[2] in Table VII.3. The full analysis should be examined in the various computation sheets presented in the companion IPA website.

In this case, the extra complications of the additional initial equity (establishment fees) and the final penalty are obviously contrived in order to illustrate the general treatment of similar front and back end expenses.

---

1. And other countries under the UK-sphere of influence.
2. Some financing bells and whistles (establishment fees and prepayment penalties) are now added since, from chapters IV and V, the reader should be able to handle their treatment.

Table VII.3 Rozy's specification sheet

Total Initial Purchase Price	100,000$
Building's initial Value	70,000$
Land's initial Value	20,000$
Plants initial Value (declining balance @30%)	10,000$
Debt to Value ratio	80%
Mortgage Loan	80,000$
Nominal Rate	6%
Amortisation	15 years
Loan establishment fees	600 $
Prepayment penalty	2 month interest
Investor's Marginal Tax Rate	48.7%
Discount rate used in the NPV_e calculation (k_e)	10%
Resale Value (10 times the NOI in year 6)	121,008$
Transaction costs	4%
Method used to calculate taxable capital gain	discount at 50%
Initial Potential Gross Income	15,000$
Gross Income Growth Rate	5%
Initial Operating Expenses	5,250$
Operating Expenses Growth Rate	3%
Vacancy Rate	5%

3. Calculating equity flows

Both the 'tax route' and the 'cash flow route' need to be retraced here:

• Along the 'tax route', the elements needed to establish a profit and loss statement are computed, as well as the yearly income tax due on rental income derived from the Rozy Building.

• As for the 'cash flow route', it allows us to determine residual cash flows once mortgage payments are met and the tax bill[1] settled.

The same distinction will then be illustrated for the disposal flows.

3.1 The tax route

From a Potential Gross Income (PGI) of 15,000$, deduct a vacancy and bad debts loss of 750$, then 5,250$ in operating expenses (OE) to obtain a Net Operating Income (NOI) of 9,000$.

---

1. Of course taxes are not paid at the end of the period, nor are rents paid as a yearly annuity. By convention and for simplicity's sake, we will treat all the flows as end of the period flows.

For tax purposes, the loan establishment fees (spread over 5 years = 120 $) and the interest portion of the mortgage payments (INT = 4,708 $) are deductible. The plant depreciation and the building deductions are equal to 4,750$ for the first year which brings us a negative taxable income of 578$ and thus a tax deduction of 281$.

If the investor's marginal tax rate remains 48.7% throughout the building's holding period,[1] his property related tax payments should amount to 1,860$ in the fourth year and 2,451 $ in the last year.(figure VII.3)

Figure VII.3 Down the tax route

PGI	2,003.00 $
VAC	17,364.38 $
EGI	-15,361.38 $
OE	16,496.16 $
NOI	5,736.82 $
Interest on debt	4,708 $
Loan establishement	120 $
Depreciation	4,750 $
Taxable income	-578 $
Operation taxes	-281 $

3.2 The cash flow route

To compute cash flows - you deduct the entire mortgage payment (8,101 $) from the NOI in order to obtain the before-tax cash flows. The last step is to deduct tax due (-277 $) which leaves a 1,176 $ cash flow in the investor's pocket. (see figure VII-4)

---

1. Another tolerable simplification. Actually the effective marginal rate of taxation will be affected by the operation and even more notably by the disposal of the investment. In real life, a complete analysis of this variation should be undertaken.

Figure VII.4 Down the cash flow route

PGI	15,000 $
VAC	750 $
EGI	14,250 $
OE	5,250 $
NOI	9,000 $
PMT	8,101 $
BTCF	899 $
Taxes	-281.34 $
ATCF	1,180 $

3.3 Allocating the operating flows

Now we may allocate the net income streams among the three groups of players in the investment game. First the mortgage payments go to the debt holder, next income tax is channelled to the Tax person, and whatever is left goes to the investor in the form of after-tax cash flows (ATCF).

Here is how the flows will be shared among the different players over the five years of operation:

Table VII.4 The Rozy Building, Who gets What?

	Years	1	2	3	4	5
Property	Net Operating Income	9,000$	9,555$	10,141$	10,759$	11,412$
Lender	Mortgage Payments	8,101$	8,101$	8,101$	8,101$	8,101$
Tax authority	Taxes on Operations	-281$	529 $	1,230$	1,860$	2,451$
Investor	After-Tax Cash Flows	1,180$	925$	810$	798$	860$

For the whole holding period the operations can be summarised again in the following table and trees.

Table VII.5 Rozy's five years of operation

Years of operation	1998	1999	2000	2001	2002	2003
Potential Gross Income	15 000 $	15 750 $	16 538 $	17 364 $	18 233 $	19 144 $
Vacancies and bad debts	750 $	788 $	827 $	868 $	912 $	957 $
Effective gross income	14 250 $	14 963 $	15 711 $	16 496 $	17 321 $	18 187 $
Operating expenses	5 250 $	5 408 $	5 570 $	5 737 $	5 909 $	6 086 $
Net Operating Income	**9 000 $**	**9 555 $**	**10 141 $**	**10 759 $**	**11 412 $**	**12 101 $**
Interest	4 708 $	4 498 $	4 276 $	4 040 $	3 790 $	
Total debt service	8 101 $	8 101 $	8 101 $	8 101 $	8 101 $	
Before-tax cash flows	**899 $**	**1 454 $**	**2 040 $**	**2 658 $**	**3 311 $**	
Depreciation	4 750 $	3 850 $	3 220 $	2 779 $	2 470 $	
Establishment fees	120 $	120 $	120 $	120 $	120 $	
Taxable income	- 578 $	1 087 $	2 525 $	3 820 $	5 032 $	
Taxes on operation	- 281 $	529 $	1 230 $	1 860 $	2 451 $	
After-tax cash flows	**1 180 $**	**925$**	**810 $**	**798 $**	**860 $**	

4. Calculating disposal cash flows

Upon disposal, the proceeds from the sale (or from any other form of disposal) will be divided among the same actors following the financial and fiscal rules described in Chapters IV and V.

4.1 Analysing disposition via the tax route

Recall the two fiscal consequences of disposal that were illustrated at the end of chapter V in the Rozy example: capital gain and depreciation balancing adjustment.

— Capital gains realised on the disposal of buildings and land is taxable. The cost base of the building will be decreased by the accumulated deductions on capital works.

— Should the net disposal price be greater than the undepreciated cost of depreciable assets, the accumulated depreciation will be recaptured and will be added to the investor's taxable income (and conversely). This balancing adjustment is added (or deducted) fully from the taxpayer income and thus taxed at the marginal rate (With Rozy since the depreciable assets were sold - very conveniently - exactly at the adjustable balance, we do not have any balancing adjustment.

Figure VII.5 Disposition tax route

Gross disposition	121,009 $
Transaction costs	4,840 $
Net disposal (total)	116,169 $
Net disposal of depreciable assets	1,681 $
Net disposal land and building	114,488 $
Taxable capital gain	16,315 $
Taxable balancing adjustment	0 $
Taxable amount at disposal	16,315 $
Taxes to be paid at disposal	7,945 $

4.2 Disposition via the cash flow route

The 'cash flow route' is a short one: from a gross disposal price of 121,008 $, we need only subtract transaction costs (*i.e.*, 4% of TC = 4,840 $), the outstanding mortgage balance (60,807 $ at the end of year five) plus the pre-payment penalty of 608 $, and pay the ATO claim of 7,945 $. This leaves 46,808 $ in the investor's pocket. This amount is referred to as After-Tax Equity on Disposal (ATED).

Figure VII.6: Disposition cash flow route

| Gross disposition | 121,009 $ |

| Transaction costs | 0 $ |

| Net disposal (total) | 121,009 $ |

| Outstanding balance and penalties | 61,415 $ |

| Before tax equity residual | 54,753 $ |

| Taxes to be paid at disposal | 7,945 $ |

| After tax equity residual | 46,808 $ |

4.3 The allocation of disposal flows

As before, the Net Disposition Price is dealt among the three partners. The outstanding mortgage balance and a penalty reverts to the Bank, taxes to the Queen and the remainder is left to the investor (*i.e.*, 61,415$, 7,945$ and 46,808$ respectively).

We can now combine the operations and disposal analyses to draw Rozy's whole financial picture in table VII.6 which should, by now, be self-explanatory.

Table VII.6 Operations and disposal flows (in dollars)

		Operations					Disposal	
Years		1	2	3	4	5		
Debt holder	PMT	8,101	8,101	8,101	8,101	8,101	OSB + Penalty	61,415
Tax person	TAXOP	-281	529	1,230	1,860	2,451	TAXDIS	7,945
Investor	ATCF	1,180	925	810	798	860	ATED	46,808
Total	NOI	9,000	9,555	10,141	10,759	11,412	NDP	116,168

5. Valuing the investment

For our present purpose, we focus on the third line of Table VII.6, that is, the five-year stream of after-tax cash flows (ATCF) and the last year's after-tax disposal flow (ATED) left in the investor's pocket in exchange for his initial 20,600$ equity investment (20,000$ + establishment fees). Since these flows are spread over a five-year period they must be discounted back to the first year and expressed as a single measurement: the net present value of the equity investment. The size and occurrence of these flows can be seen below.

Figure VII.7

```
                              Disposal Equity Flow: 46,808 $
                                              ↑
              ↑        ↑       ↑       ↑       ↑
           1,180$    925$    810$    798$    860$

    ↓
Initial Equity Investment: 20,600$
```

These cash flows (both ATCF and ATED) must be discounted using a rate that best reflects the after-tax rate of return normally expected on investment with similar financial risk levels and blend of operations, location, taxation and managerial characteristics. This rate of return on equity is noted k_e and, for the time being, let us proceed as if k_e were known to the investor.

We now compare the present value of the operation and disposal flows with the initial equity investment. A present value in excess of the equity investment indicates that the investor's rate of return is greater than k_e. In this case the Rozy investment beats the expected target of 10%. Needless to say, a negative net present value signifies a rate of return less than k_e and indicates that the project should not be undertaken under present conditions.

We should even be able to find the highest price our investor should bid for the building and still earn no less than his anticipated return, k_e. Let's go through the steps once again (see also Table VII.6).

Assuming $k_e = 10\%$, the present value becomes:

$$PV = \frac{ATCF_1}{(1+k_e)^1} + \frac{ATCF_2}{(1+k_e)^2} + \frac{ATCF_3}{(1+k_e)^3} + \frac{ATCF_4}{(1+k_e)^4} + \frac{ATCF_5}{(1+k_e)^5} + \frac{ATER_5}{(1+k_e)^5}$$

PV = 32,589 $

The investment's net present value is found by subtracting the initial equity investment ($E_0 = 20,600\$$) from the present value:

NPV = 32,589$ - 20,600$

NPV = **11,989$**

The net present value is the expected extra 'reward' for investing in this project instead of investing elsewhere at 10%. In other words, not only will our investor earn a 10% return on his investment but he increases his wealth by **11,989$**.

Since he must borrow 80,000$ to launch the project, the investor should not offer more than 112,589 $ (80,000$ in debt and 32,589$ in present value). This **Maximum Bidding Price** is also called the **Justified Investment Price (JIP)**. At that ceiling price, a 32,589 $ outlay would earn him exactly 10%. Should the sale close at a lower price, his return rises and conversely.

In a real-life transaction, the buyer and the vendor will probably reach a price below the Maximum Bid Price. The investor's return will of course depend on the closing price and, his inner voice will tell him:

> 'If I pay 112,589$ for Rozy, a 32,589$ equity should yield a 10% return... not bad, but since I don't want to put down more than 20,000$[1], I'd better negotiate. With a final offer of 100,000$ (a 80,000$ mortgage loan and 20,000$ cash down payment) my return will surely be higher than 10% seeing that I get a 11 989$ net present value. Indeed, I will get a 21.27% internal rate of return on equity... not too bad!'

And, for one last time, we could graph the value determination:

Figure VII.8

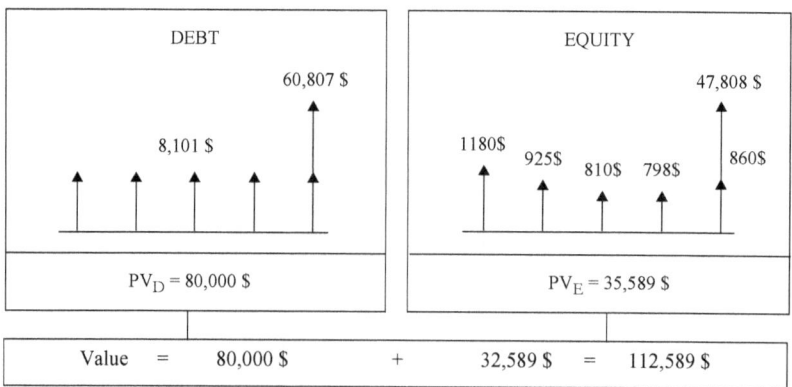

---

[1]. The mortgage establishment fees should be added to the initial cash. They are neglected here to have a simpler story. The effect on return is negligible.

6. Conclusion

Through abundant repetition of earlier chapter material and a simple example, we have managed to round up all the major principles needed to correctly assess the investment value of any property.

In Liechtenstein, and for all nontaxable investors, we must discount before-tax cash flows (BTCF) using the tax-free rate of return (k_e*). Given that this rate is lower than the equivalent taxable expected rate, non taxable institutions should, in principle, attach a higher price than would their taxable competitors to the same stream of net operating income flows.

Furthermore, if one has no debt, the expected rate should be lower yet ($k_e = k_a$) and should in fact resemble the going rate on other non levered financial instruments (shares, bonds, etc.). Acknowledging that the discount rate varies according to fiscal and debt status raises the slippery problem of market stratification and clientele effects:

— investors in a high tax bracket are inclined to invest in assets favoured by financial gearing and depreciation shelters (direct property assets);

— minimally taxed or entirely untaxed investors prefer to accumulate assets bearing little fiscal protection (*e.g.*, land assets) or in assets that allow the pass-through of property tax advantages (*e.g.*, listed property trusts).

Though we cannot expand upon this complex and little understood problem, we can at least encourage reflection on the concept of value, and how bid prices are determined by the comparison of the yields offered on all forms of investment.

The investor should always keep in mind that:

1. The Maximum Bidding Price (MBP) depends on the k_e discount rate chosen by the equity owner based on his own preferences, his fiscal status and other investment possibilities he may be considering. This process is at least partly subjective and explains why no single MBP exists and, as a direct consequence, why the concept of 'investment value' becomes so blurred.

2. The valuation exercise relies on forecasts of both net revenues and net disposal price. The price and returns derived obviously stand on no more ground than the forecasts which underlie them... unless they were endowed with most enviable oracular powers, analysts are unable to predict with perfect foresight how the Rozy Building will perform. That is another reason why you need not fuss over the precision of your calculations, and once again, accept the fuzziness of the 'value' concept.

3. When comparing Property with other financial instruments, keep in mind that the present values and the discount rates calculated are **after-debt and**

after-tax on a investment typically using financial gearing under operating conditions not found in other types of investment and under particular but contingent tax treatments.

Very few, if any, alternative investments have the same 'risk-illiquidity - leverage - tax gimmicks - opacity - management - mythological value - location dependence - political sensitivity - immutability - longevity' bundle of traits as Property investments.

Thus, in view of these caveats, let us cease our endless parlour squabbles over how one's Property investments compare with Aunt Gertrude's stock portfolio or Mr. Pedro's Renoir collection!

Chapter VIII

Property risk analysis

Where we take a second look at our assumption of certainty and learn to adjust our models accordingly. Where we simulate investment risks and evaluate the consequences. Where, lastly, we get to play roulette.

Though the concept of risk permeates all previous chapters, it has for good reasons been kept fairly vague. We had a rather intuitive notion of risk and the risk-return relationship, one that acknowledged that risk takers should be compensated for their inconvenience. As it turns out, this intuitive conception of risk is correct and underlies most of modern investment theory. Indeed, we have used it so pervasively that we may have forgotten that we have neither defined nor properly analysed the risk elements to be dealt with in real estate analysis.

Not only must we define and identify the main sources of risk, we must also strive to quantify it and, in some way, work it to our decision models. Having spent the better part of the previous chapter elaborating decision rules to fit a world of certainty, we must step back and make sure our models can be tuned and adapted to fit the very uncertain world in which we live and value assets.

1. Risk taking: defined and dissected

1.1 Risk and uncertainty

Both terms have been used quite loosely so far, but we could not try to distinguish 'risk' from 'uncertainty'. Uncertainty is the admission of total ignorance about possible outcomes. In an 'uncertain' environment the analyst has to keep in mind that anything can happen: a revolution, major revamping of the tax laws or an erratic blimp in market behaviour. Uncertainty is the background of all decisions but cannot be incorporated explicitly into the decision rules: there are no useful forecasting tools to deal with uncertainty, only forecasting fools…

Riskiness implies some form of *a priori* knowledge about the range of possible occurrences and is defined as a degree of variability. The riskiness of an asset (or a project, or a property) is defined as the probable variability of future cash flows to be derived from this asset; the more variable the cash flows, the 'riskier' the asset. For instance, an industrial building leased year by year to a computer software company is riskier than an office building bound by a twenty-year lease with the federal government. We should emphasize that a risky project can mean bad news or good news: the software company might go belly up, but it could also turn into a prime tenant. Conversely, a riskless project means 'no news', bad or good: the variation range of expected outcomes is much narrower.

1.2 Dissecting risk

1.2.1 General risk and specific risk

General risk is external to the specific investment. We ascribe it to the operation of the market as a whole and/or the economy as a whole. It also goes under the names of 'market risk' and 'systematic risk'. Since all investments are, to a certain extent, dependent on the vagaries of the economy, one cannot escape general risk through diversification. Putting one's proverbial eggs in many baskets would serve little purpose if the baskets were placed on the same cart...

Specific risk is unique to a particular asset or class of assets: it results from the idiosyncrasy of a given investment. Other names for this concept include 'residual risk' and 'unsystematic risk'. Since each investment carries its own specific risk, some protection can be obtained through diversification. A portfolio of properties spreads out the risk specific to each particular property, just as carting several egg-baskets still beats carting one big one.

Figure VIII.1

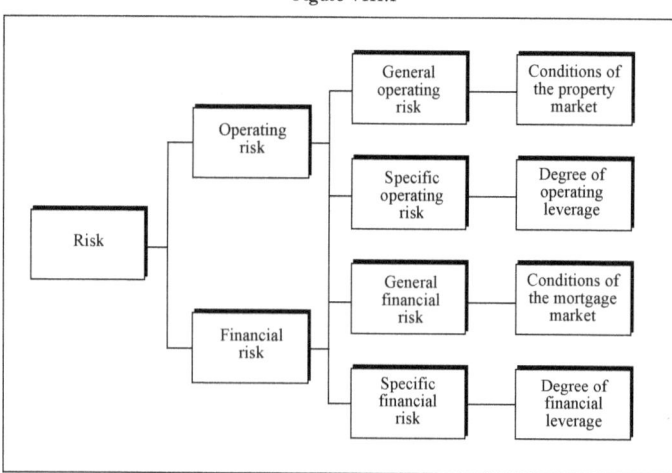

Figure VIII.2

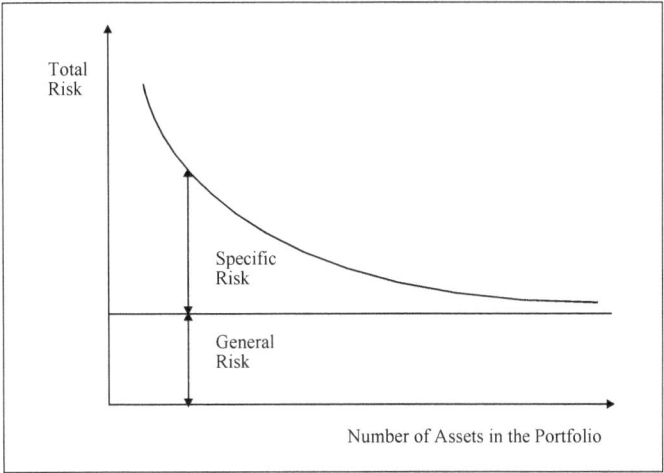

1.2.2 Business risks and financial risks

Business risks can be general or specific. General business risks, say in Real Estate, result from the supply and demand conditions on the real estate markets. Specific business risks are related to a property's operating characteristics, to its operating leverage. They may also be related to insurable physical hazards.

Financial risks also fall under general and specific headings. General financial risks arise from the supply and demand conditions on the financial markets. Specific financial risks are linked to particular financing underlying a property, its financial leverage.

This chapter deals mainly with specific business and financial risk. These sources of risk are easy to identify and quantify as both derive from investment particulars (operating and financial leverage).

1.3 Exposure to business and financial risk

Specific business risk evokes visions of physical calamities: fire, floods and mud slides. Such events may be 'uncertain' (unpredictable) for most individual owners but they become a 'risk' for insurance companies. Their probability of occurring is well documented, so fee schedules have been drawn up to distribute such risks among a very large pool of policyholders. By taking out an insurance policy, a property owner is relieved of the possibility of a huge loss should a calamity strike and settles for the assured payment of a predictable annual premium. This premium merely adds to fixed operating costs.

Exposure to business risk also depends on the property's operating leverage, *i.e.*, the relationship between fixed costs, variable costs and net operating income. In a previous chapter, we saw how the higher the share of fixed costs, the higher the NOI must be to cover both fixed and variable costs; in other words, the higher the break-even point.

The Degree of Operating Leverage (DOL) is an indicator of risk exposure to a variation in rental revenue. It is a structural indicator of business risk. A more 'elastic' operating structure (*i.e.*, with a large share of fixed costs) is riskier because, on the down side, a drop in occupancy is more likely to mean trouble. However, on the upside, a hike in the rate yields impressive operating results. Again, greater potential for returns is earned at the expense of a higher risk level.

> DOL = (ΔNOI/NOI) /(Δn/n)
>
> The percentage change in NOI divided by the percentage change in occupancy gives us the Degree of Operating Leverage.

Exposure to specific financial risk is related to the property's capital structure: the relationship between debt and equity. The degree of financial leverage (DFL) gives us an indication of the elasticity of cash flows with respect to changes in net operating income. The larger the share of debt in the capital structure, the higher the NOI must be to cover the debt service, thus the higher the debt coverage point.

> DFL = (ΔCF/CF) /ΔNOI/NOI)
>
> The percentage change in cash flows divided by the percentage change in net operating income gives us the Degree of Financial Leverage.

Finally, we can combine these two ratios to get a Degree of Total Leverage (DTL) expressing the simultaneous effect of operating and financial leverage. Here's how:

DTL = Degree of Operating Leverage × Degree of Financial Leverage

DTL = (DNOI/NOI)/(Dn/n) × (DCF/CF)/(DNOI/NOI)

which boils down to:

> DTL = (ΔCF/CF)/(Δn/n)

Figure VIII.3 shows how these ratios tie in together and Table VIII.1 gives an example. Here, the degree of financial leverage is calculated, as in most textbooks, on Before-Tax Cash Flows. It would, however, be more appropriate to use an After-Tax measurement since the financing structure may strongly affect the taxation situation of the investor.

Figure VIII.3

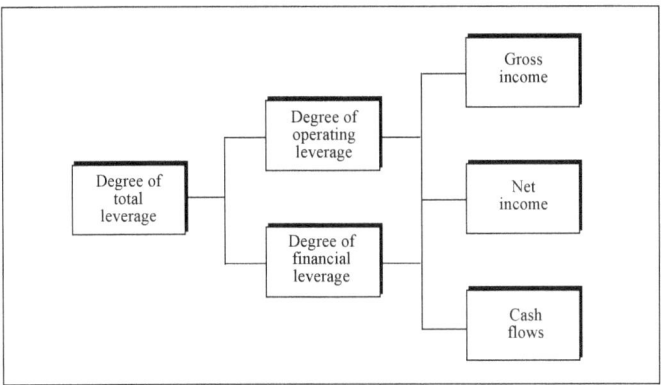

Table VIII.1   Leverage on Octavus

Rent per unit	rpu	1,000 $			
Number of units	n	20			
Variable costs per unit	vcu	300 $			
Fixed costs	FC	4,000 $			
Property value	V	100,000 $			
Mortgage	D	80,000 $			
Mortgage rate		8%			
Depreciation		25			
Number of occupied units		5	14	18	20
Effective gross income		5,000 $	14,000 $	18,000 $	20,000 $
Variable costs		1500 $	4,200 $	5,400 $	6,000 $
Fixed costs		4,000 $	4,000 $	4,000 $	4,000 $
Operating expenses		5,500 $	8,200 $	9,400 $	10,000 $
Net operating income		- 500 $	5,800 $	8,600 $	10,000 $
Mortgage payment		7,409 $	7,409 $	7,409 $	7,409 $
Degree of Operating Leverage		-7	1.69	1.47	1.40
Degree of Financial Leverage		0.06	-3.60	7.22	3.86
Degree of Total Leverage		-0.44	-6.09	10.58	5.40
Break even point		16.30	16.30	16.30	16.30

These ratios take us a step ahead in estimating an asset's riskiness and enable us to give an opinion as to how our investment will behave under various market situations. Although we cannot predict the direction in which variations will occur, at least we know the range in which they will fall. For the rest of the chapter we will assume that knowing a building's operating and financial leverage will allow us to establish its risk level. Now let us determine that risk-level and include it in our analysis.

2. Risk measurement

2.1 Probability distributions

Most real estate investment decisions and valuation exercises involve a forecast of expected cash flows and reversion values. In previous chapters, these forecasted flows were confidently accepted as point estimates: we had a single, precise figure for each flow and each reversion value.

One would have to be particularly foolhardy to stake a project's viability on the exact fulfilment of point estimates. Practitioners know how predicting next week's interest rates is a challenge, so how can we even aspire to precision in five-year forecasts? At best, a seasoned investor will venture an opinion on the probable distribution of key variables: rates, rents, prices, etc. She is then able to test how her investment will perform in different market situations. To clarify this mental process, let us look at the simple example shown in Table VIII.2, where monthly rents are estimated in three market situations.

Table VIII.2   Expected monthly rent in different market situations

Market situation	Monthly rents
Strong market	1,200 $
Average market	1,000 $
Slow market	800 $

At first sight, this matching of monthly rents to market situations may seem trivial, yet it is a clear improvement over our earlier point estimates. We now have an idea of the span of the monthly rents and a clue as to the risk this investment entails. We could further refine our analysis by attributing probabilities to each one of the market situations. Obviously, these probabilities are subjective and depend on each person's feelings about where the market is heading. Then again, these feelings are precisely those on which investors base their decisions.

Let's meet three investors, Mr. Bland, Ms Optima and Mr. Pessim and see how they view the investment's prospects:

— Mr. Bland walks the middle way and assigns an equal chance to each of the three market situations: each one is weighted by a probability of 1/3;

— Ms Optima lives in a rosier world and feels the market has a 70% chance of being 'strong', a 20% chance of being 'average' and a 10% chance of being 'slow';

— Mr. Pessim, you guessed it, assigns probabilities of 10%, 30% and 60% respectively for each market situation.

On the basis of these probability distributions we can derive the expected values shown in Table VIII.3 by multiplying the anticipated monthly rents by the probability each investor assigned to the occurrence of each market situation and summing these expected values.

Table VIII.3 Calculation of the expected values

Market situation	Anticipated Monthly Rent	Probabilities and Expected Values According to Three Investors					
		Mr. Bland		Ms Optima		Mr. Pessim	
		Probability	Expected Values	Probability	Expected Values	Probability	Expected Values
Strong	1,200 $	0.33	396	0.70	840	0.10	120
Average	1,000 $	0.33	330	0.20	200	0.30	300
Slow	800 $	0.33	264	0.10	80	0.60	480
Expected Values of Monthly Rents			990		1,120		900

By following this exercise, each investor can distil his anticipations as to monthly rents (denoted v_i) and the probabilities attached to the occurrence of each market situation (p_i) into a single indicator - the expected value of monthly rents (denoted $E(V)$). We can formalize this reasoning as follows:

$$E(V) = p_1 \times V_1 + p_2 \times V_2 + p_3 \times V_3$$
$$E(V) = S\, p_i \times V_i$$

We can go on to use this indicator in comparing investment alternatives confronting an investor, say Ms Optima. Let us imagine that she maintains her anticipations regarding the coming performance of the rental market and is now trying to choose between projects A and B. Assuming her optimism hasn't faded since we were first introduced to her, she could be using Table VIII.4 to enlighten her decision making.

Table VIII.4 Ms Optima compares two rental projects

Rental Market Situation	Associated Probability	Project A (in $)		Project B (in $)	
		Monthly Rent	Expected Values	Monthly Rent	Expected Values
Strong	0.70	1 200	840	1 400	980
Average	0.20	1 000	200	500	100
Slow	0.10	800	80	400	40
			1 120		1 120

Faced with these results, Ms Optima must conclude that project B is riskier than project A even though the expected pays-off are identical. After all, Ms Optima may be optimistic, but, as all investors, she has an aversion to risk. She will, therefore, go ahead with project A since she can get the same expected return while exposing herself to less risk.

In presenting Ms Optima's world, we oversimplified the issue by supposing only three market situations could occur (strong, average and slow). Of course, a more ambitious analyst might prefer to introduce more subtle shades into the picture, (let's say: vibrant, strong, healthy, average, faltering, slow, comatose) and probabilities would have to be assigned to each of these, resulting in a more complex pay-off table.

Were this analyst not only ambitious but also smart, she might even conceive a continuum of market situations, increasing ever so smoothly from comatose to vibrant, and give us, in more formal terms, a continuous probability distribution. This would be a useful move toward simplifying our analysis since these distributions are handily drawn as curves whose shape gives a good clue as to the risk involved. Figure VIII.4 shows how this smart analyst would depict the probability distributions relative to projects A and B.

Figure VIII.4

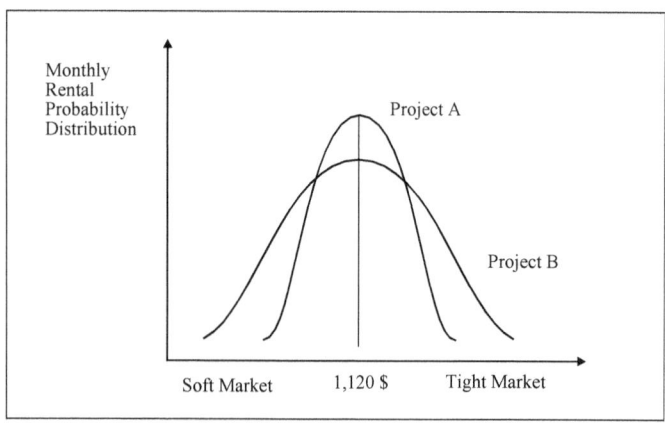

Once again we note both projects have identical expected values but that the chance of earning greater rents is higher in project A. Understandably, our smart and risk-shy investor will side with project A.

Project A holds fewer surprises (good or bad) than B. The rents eventually earned in A are more likely to centre around the expected value since the distribution is visibly narrower or less dispersed, as it were. To assist us in quantifying risk, let us now draw on the idea of dispersion.

2.2 Measuring dispersion and assessing risk

The narrowness or compactness or a probability distribution can be measured with traditional statistical instruments: variance, standard deviation and variation coefficients. These should be familiar to most readers and we can use them to compare two hypothetical projects: a shopping centre and an office building. For the time being, we will contrive a very simple world: one where, according to our analyst Mr. Ikeda, the Tokyo leasing market stands at a 20%, 40% and 40% chance respectively of turning poor, fair or good.

Table VIII.5   How two real estate projects fare on the Tokyo market (000 000 ¥)

Market Situation	Associated Probability	Net Operating Income (NOI)		Deviation from Expected NOI	Standard Deviation	Variance
	p_i	NOI_i	$p_i \cdot NOI_i$	$(NOI_i - \overline{NOI_i})$	$(NOI_i - \overline{NOI_i})^2$	$p_i \cdot (NOI_i - \overline{NOI_i})^2$
(1)	(2)	(3)	(4)	(5)	(6)	(7)
Office Building						
Poor	0.20	100	20	(60)	3 600	720
Fair	0.40	150	60	(10)	100	40
Good	0.40	200	80	40	1 600	640
Expected Value			160			
Variance (σ^2)						1 400
Standard Deviation (σ)						37.42
Variation Coefficient ($\sigma/\overline{NOI_i}$)						0.23
Shopping Centre						
Poor	0.20	80	16	(80)	6 400	1 280
Fair	0.40	100	40	(60)	3 600	1 440
Good	0.40	260	104	100	10 000	4 000
Expected Value			160			
Variance (σ^2)						6 720
Standard Deviation (σ)						81.98
Variation Coefficient ($\sigma/\overline{NOI_i}$)						0.51

Let us review Table VIII.5 together.

— Columns 1 to 3 list the various market situations and how each project responds to them. The office building (leased to AAA tenants) rides market swings quite smoothly, with NOI going from 100 to 200 million ¥ while the shopping centre's NOI dips as low as 80 million ¥ and peaks at 260 million ¥. Here, as is usually the case in reality, the office building's prospects are more stable - less risky - than the shopping centre's.

— The expected values shown in column 4 are the product of Ikeda San's anticipated NOIs and the probability he assigned to each market situation.

The 160 million ¥ amount appearing at the bottom of the column is simply the sum of the individual expected values and, as such, constitutes the project's overall expected value. Subtracting the expected value for each market situation from the overall expected value gives us the amounts in column 5. Column 6 shows the squares of these deviations, while column 7 weighs each of these by the appropriate probability. Summing column 7 gives the distribution's variance (denoted s^2) and extracting the square root yields the standard deviation (s). The standard deviation - given in millions of Yen - can be normalized and expressed as a percentage, the variation coefficient, by dividing it by the project's expected value.

Now we can put some hard figures on our vague concepts of riskiness. The shopping centre has an 81.98 million ¥ standard deviation around its 160 million ¥ expected value. The office building shows a 37.42 million ¥ standard deviation around the same expected value. Hence, we can conclude that the shopping centre is approximately twice as risky as the office building.

The same information is also conveyed by the coefficient of variation (51% and 23%, respectively) which measures the amount of risk per unit of return (in this case, per yen). This feature is particularly useful when the expected values differ and when comparing investment projects of different sizes.

Summing up the analysis

	Office Building	Shopping Centre
In Millions of ¥		
Expected Value	160	160
Variance (σ^2)	1 400	6 720
Standard Deviation (σ)	37.42	81.98
Variation Coefficient (%)	23%	51%

Yoku dekimashita Ikeda San!

However, Mr. Ikeda would surely concede that the 'real' world - even more so in Tokyo! - is far too complex to be reduced to a 'poor - fair - good' description. Rather, he would likely resort to a probability distribution such as the normal (or Gaussian) distribution. We might as well follow suit: after all, normal curves are presented in neat little tables at the end of most textbooks. If that were not reason enough, statisticians assure us that most random events can indeed be represented by a normal distribution. In short, unless you have very good reasons to choose another probabilistic model, you are always better off referring to the normal distribution.

Once you know the mean and the standard deviation of any normal distribution (for example on the NOI), you can convert it into a standardized 'unit-less' Z distribution, which can be obtained by the following transformations:

$$Z = \frac{NOI_i - \overline{NOI}_i}{\sigma}$$

Under its Z form, the standardized curve of net operating income is readily interpreted as a given number of standard deviations away from the mean, as illustrated in Figure VIII.5. The normal distribution of a continuous variable can always be transformed into a standardized form where Z is normally distributed with a mean of zero and a variance of 1.

Consider the points marked $z = 1$, $z = 2$, $z = 3$ and their mirror equivalents $z = -1$, $z = -2$, $z = -3$ (*i.e.*, 1, 2 & 3 standard deviations away from the mean). Each set of points delimits an area covering 68.27%, 95.45% and 99.74% respectively, of the total area under the curve. Suppose net operating income fits a normal distribution having a mean of 100$ and a 15$ standard deviation and you wish to estimate the probability, that net operating income will in fact fall within 80$ and 130$.

Figure VIII.5

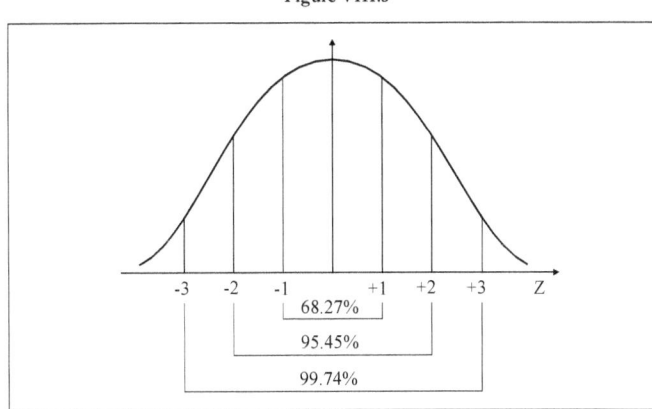

The first step is to change the boundaries into their Z equivalents:

$$Z_{80} = \frac{NOI_i - \overline{NOI}_i}{\sigma} = \frac{80 - 100}{15} = -1.33$$

$$Z_{130} = \frac{NOI_i - \overline{NOI}_i}{\sigma} = \frac{130 - 100}{15} = 2$$

The probabilities can be read off a standardized normal distribution table as the areas found under the curve.

The area between -1.33 and 0 (the left half of the curve) accounts for 40.82% of the distribution, while the area found between 2 and 0 (the right half) amounts to 47.72%. Since the area extending between -1.33 and 2 covers 88.54% of the entire area under the curve, we are led to conclude that there is an 88.54% probability of net operating income falling within the 80$ to 130$ target we are investigating.

Figure VIII.6

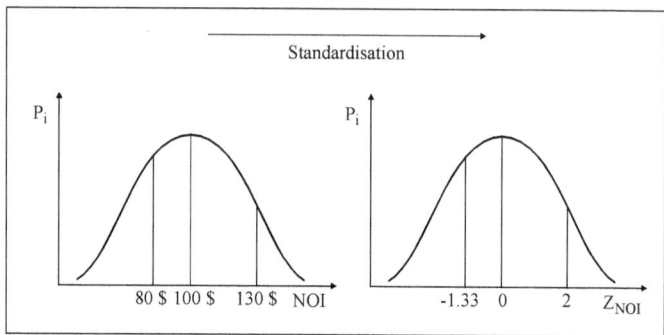

Following this same line of reasoning, the investor may well ask his question differently: what is the probability that the net operating income exceeds 80$, 100$ or 150$? The cumulated probability distribution shown below would provide the answer.

Table VIII.6   Cumulated probability distribution of NOI_i

NOI_i	Z value	Probability that NOI is larger than NOI_i
80	-1.33	0.9082
100	0	0.5000
120	1.33	0.0918
130	2	0.0228
150	3.33	0.0000

In the following illustration, we would like to put a real estate analyst into a quasi-realistic situation. Imagine she invested 30,000 $ equity into a three-year project with the after-tax cash flows, the reversion values and the probability distribution of market situations listed in Table VIII.7. Note how, for some odd reason, our analyst (Ms Optima again) varies the weights assigned to each market situation from year to year, becoming increasingly optimistic as the project unfolds. But, unwilling to fuss over statistical niceties, she assumes that the project's net present value will be normally distributed.

As indicated in Table VIII.7, when the equity flows are discounted at 5%, the resulting expected net present value is 6,316$. By computing the variance and standard deviation (s = 2,695 $) we can derive the matching Z distribution and go on to determine the point on the curve that reduces the net present value to zero. That point is found in this manner:

$$Z_{NPV} = \frac{0 - \overline{NPV}}{\sigma_{NPV}} = \frac{0 - 6,316\$}{2,695\$} = -2.34$$

Figure VIII.7

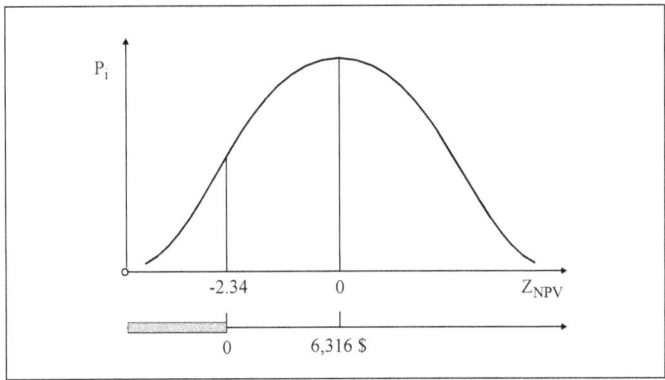

The numbers speak for themselves (or almost!).

The odds of losing out on this project, *i.e.*, the probability of incurring a negative net present value, is only 0.96% (the area under the curve excluded by a -2.34 Z score). Obviously, our analyst, now exhausted by all the mental gymnastics, will have found peace of mind and need no longer fret over this project.

Partial conclusion:

Risk and uncertainty are the lot of all investors and promoters, and hence they must be incorporated into their decision models. Some sources of uncertainty lie beyond the reach of rational investors: these are better left to astrologers. Some can be transferred to other economic agents and are better left to insurance companies. Finally, some specific sources of risk can be assessed by considering both operating and financial structural characteristics (the degrees of operating and financial leverage). Starting from these and making some subjective judgement on where the markets are heading, we can derive the probability distributions describing the investment's performance (net operating income, net present value, etc.). Finally, we saw how, with the aid of simple statistical tools (measures of dispersion), we can assess and compare the risk levels of competing investments.

Table VIII.7

State of the Economy	First Year p_i^1	$ATCF_i^1$	$p_i^1 \cdot ATCF_i^1$	Second Year p_i^2	$ATCF_i^2$	$p_i^2 \cdot ATCF_i^2$	Third Year p_i^3	$ATCF_i^3$	$p_i^3 \cdot ATCF_i^3$	Year of Disposal p_i^3	ATDF	$p_i^3 \cdot ATDF$
Poor	0.5	1,000 $	500 $	0.2	1,200 $	240 $	0.1	1,500 $	150 $	0.1	30,000 $	3,000 $
So-so	0.3	1,200 $	360 $	0.5	1,400 $	700 $	0.4	1,800 $	720 $	0.4	36,000 $	14,400 $
Good	0.2	1,500 $	300 $	0.3	1,600 $	480 $	0.5	2,000 $	1,000 $	0.5	40,000 $	20,000 $
ATCF expected values			1,160 $			1,420 $			1,870 $			37,400 $
NPV = −30,000 $	+		$1,160/(1.05)^1$	+		$1,420/(1.05)^2$	+		$1,870/(1.05)^3$	+		$37,400/(1.05)^3$

NPV at 5% = 6,316 $

	Deviation*	Squared deviation	Variance	Deviation	Squared deviation	Variance	Deviation	Squared deviation	Variance	Deviation	Squared deviation	Variance
	−160 $	25,600 $	12,800 $	−220 $	48,400 $	9,680 $	−370 $	136,900 $	13,690 $	−7,400 $	54,760,000 $	5,476,000 $
	40 $	1,600 $	480 $	−20 $	400 $	200 $	−70 $	4,900 $	1,960 $	−1,400 $	1,960,000 $	784,000 $
	340 $	115,600 $	23,120 $	180 $	32,400 $	9,720 $	130 $	16,900 $	8,450 $	2,600 $	6,760,000 $	3,380,000 $
Variance			36,400 $			19,600 $			24,100 $			9,640,000 $
Standard deviation			191 $			140 $			155 $			3,105 $
NPV variance =	+		$36,400/(1.05)^1$	+		$19,600/(1.05)^2$	+		$24,100/(1.05)^3$	+		$9,640,000/(1.05)^3$

NPV variance = 7,260,641 $
NPV standard deviation = 2,695 $

* Deviation = $NOI_i - \overline{NOI}_i$
Squared deviation = $(NOI_i - \overline{NOI}_i)^2$
Variance = $p_i \cdot (NOI_i - \overline{NOI}_i)^2$

With this extra sophistication, our analyst can add more depth to her analysis by quantifying her investment alternatives in probabilistic terms: 'the probability that the net present value be positive is ...'. This type of statement is far more convincing and reassuring than a straight point estimate. We will now see how we can further refine our treatment of risk.

3. Single project risk analysis

To analyse the risk an investment entails, we should ideally consider how the project affects the real estate assets and, eventually, all the other assets already in the hands of the decision-maker. Reviewing the entire portfolio would permit us to use the common analytical tools of general financial theory, and particularly enable us to ground our treatment of risk in the widely acknowledged Capital Asset Pricing Model (CAPM).

However, delving into these matters would take us beyond the limits of this introductory text and, on the other hand in particular, there is as yet too little evidence to corroborate the applicability of these models to real estate analysis. We will, for the time being, limit this presentation to the traditional approach when conducting single project risk analysis.

3.1 Tuning for risk

3.1.1 Makeshift methods

Despite their repeated condemnation by financial management textbooks, several inadvisable methods are still common practice... a fact which serves to prove two things: 1. That practitioners don't read textbooks (this one will be no exception), and 2. The resilience of shoddy practices if they are straight forward and seem inoffensive.

These methods include ad hoc adjustments to familiar rules of thumb such as the gross income multiplier, inflating the capitalisation rate or adding a few percentage points to the security ratio.

One common method consists of shortening the acceptable payback periods; this, of course, is tantamount to increasing the required rate of return. The riskier the project, the sooner one would wish to recuperate one's investment.

All these methods share the same shortcomings:

— They are based on vague 'guesstimates'; we can never be quite sure by how much to adjust rates, multipliers or pay back periods.

— They do not acknowledge the need to discount operating cash flows and reversion values.

By now, our reader is much too sophisticated to even consider such crude techniques; but he ought to keep them in mind as they are still quite widely used in the real estate industry.

Whether dealing with discounted cash flow methods or simpler models such as a perpetuity of the $V = NOI/R$ type, we can tune our models to incorporate risk in two ways: we can either adjust the numerator (using the certainly equivalent method) or the denominator (affecting discount rate adjustments). Let us start by taking a closer look at the latter.

3.1.2 Discount rate adjustments

Traditionally, discount rates are padded with a certain risk premium to account for the perceived riskiness of a specific real estate project. Beyond the sticky empirical problem of finding the 'right' risk premium lurks a more subtle but fundamental problem. This theoretical flaw is that padding the discount rate also introduces an unwarranted adjustment for time due to the compounding effect. This oft-unaddressed issue deserves an illustration.

Suppose we discount the after-tax equity flows (operating and disposal) of a three-year project using a 10% expected rate of return on equity. This rate actually breaks down into a 4% return on a risk-free investment and a 6% risk premium.

The project's present value is given by:

$$PV = \frac{ATCF_1}{(1+0.10)^1} + \frac{ATCF_2}{(1+0.10)^2} + \frac{ATER_3}{(1+0.10)^3}$$

Let's calculate the adjustment factors implied in the above equation.

Table VIII.8   The effect of compounding on the risk premium

Year	Effective rate	Risk-free rate	Implied Risk Premium
1	1.10	1.04	0.060
2	1.21	1.0816	0.1284
3	1.331	1.1248	0.2061

One cannot help notice that the compounding effect in the second and third years dramatically increases the size of the risk premium from 6% in the first year to 20.61% in the third. To accept such a model, we would also have to assume that the project's riskiness increases with time. Can we accept this assumption? Probably not, in the case of most real estate projects. The difficult and risky years for a new project are the initial ones. There are greater risks related to the construction period, exceeding budgeted costs, the leasing up phase and the project's initial financing. Later years are much more stable: leasing is secured, the debt-load is edging down and inflation tends to smooth out other worries. Thus, in real estate, as in demography, infant mortality is the prime contributor to the average mortality rate.

Seeing as all forms of discount rate adjustments pose this problem, a few solutions have been put forward. Adjustments to the numerator is one of them.

3.1.3 Adjusting the numerator: the certainty-equivalent approach

To avoid the compounding of the risk premium over time, we can proceed to direct adjustment of the cash flows. To better illustrate the methods, we shall draw upon some of the tools developed in earlier chapters.

The 'certainty-equivalent' method rests on the notion that the investor is indifferent to a 'risky' cash flow and a smaller 'certain' amount. For example, he is indifferent between an 'uncertain' 1,500$ and a 'certain' 1,000$. We can express the relationship between these amounts as a coefficient of adjustment (denoted a) and by using the notation ATCF* for the uncertain equivalent of a certain amount ATCF:

ATCF   =   a × ATCF*

Hence:

a   =   ATCF/ATCF*
0.66   =   1 000/1 500

If this coefficient holds for all levels of cash flow, we need only multiply them by the coefficient to obtain the 'certain equivalents'.

Since this adjustment converts uncertain cash flows into their certain equivalents, it becomes imperative to discount the resulting cash flows at a 'risk-free' rate, in other words, a lower rate than would otherwise be used in comparing risk-afflicted investments.

Many authors reject this method under the pretext that it is far too difficult to establish certainty equivalent coefficients. However, we now have at our disposal tools which help us to deal with this all too real problem. If the expected ATCFs are assumed to be normally distributed and the investor knows the mean and variance of these distributions, he can determine a certain amount ATCF* by using a value that is three standard deviations away from the expected uncertain ATCF. Recall that 3s away from the mean includes 99.74% of the normalized ATCF distribution. This can be achieved in our discounted cash flow model by using the cash flows found at 3s below the mean.

Figure VIII.8

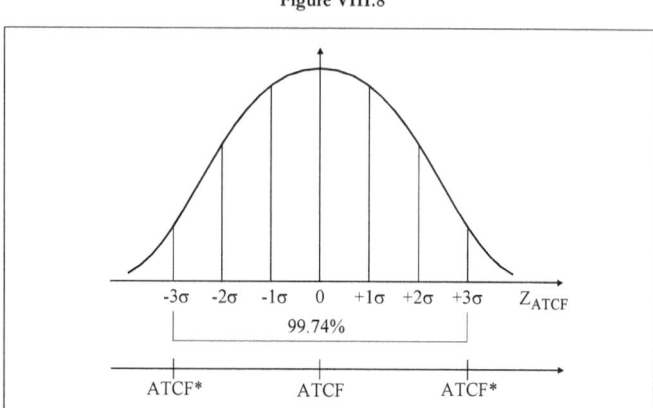

The example given in Table VIII.9 should help clarify the procedure.

Table VIII.9   A certainty equivalent application (in dollars)

Initial equity outlay	E_0	=	90 000
First year's cash flow (normal distribution with a 10,000$ mean and a 1,000$ standard deviation)	$ATCF_1$	=	N(10 000, 1 000)
Second year's cash flow (normal distribution with a 12,000$ mean and a 1,000$ standard deviation)	$ATCF_2$	=	N(12 000, 1 000)
Reversion value obtained in second year (normal distribution with a 100,000$ mean and a 5,000$ standard deviation)	ATER	=	N(100 000, 5 000)
'Risk-free' discount rate	k_f	=	4%

	$ATCF_t$	$ATCF_t^*$		α_t	PV of ATCF* at $k_f = 0.04$
0	-90 000		-90 000	1.00	-90 000.00
1	10 000	10 000 - (3 x 1 000)	= 7 000	0.70	6 730.77
2	12 000	12 000 - (3 x 1 000)	= 9 000	0.75	8 321.01
2	100 000	100 000 - (3 x 5 000)	= 85 000	0.85	78 587.28
Net Present Value of the Investment					3 639.06

Formally, this is written:

$$NPV_E = \frac{\alpha_1 \times ATCF_1}{(1+k_f)^1} + \frac{\alpha_2 \times ATCF_2}{(1+k_f)^2} + \frac{\alpha_3 \times ATER_2}{(1+k_f)^2} - E_0$$

$$NPV_E = \frac{0.70 \times 10,000\$}{(1.04)^1} + \frac{0.75 \times 12,000\$}{(1.04)^2} + \frac{0.85 \times 100,000\$}{(1.04)^2} - 90,000\$$$

$$NPV_E = 3,639.06\$$$

This example shows that our investor is 99.87% certain to increase her wealth by at least 3,639.06 $. With a z_3 score of 0.4987, there is a 49.87% chance of falling between 0 and -3 standard deviations away from the mean and likewise, a 50% probability of striking between 0 and + •, given her 99.87% odds (50% + 49.87%) of being to the right of -3 s.

Figure VIII.9

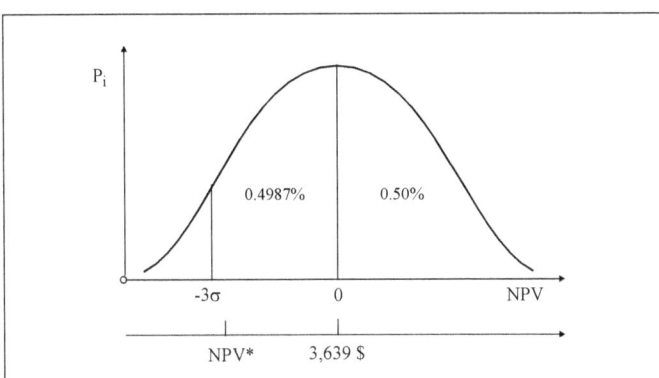

Our investor could conceivably risk a little more exposure and decide to go through the same exercise using only two or even one standard deviations below the mean. The choice of a safety margin is up to her and depends on her aversion to risk.

As we have just witnessed, the 'probabilised' certainty equivalent method is quite manageable and does not lead to the theoretical heresy committed when relying on discount rate adjustments. This author has a strong preference for this method but must grudgingly side with the opinion expressed by A. Jaffe and C.F. Sirmans:

> '...Despite the theoretical attractiveness of the certainty equivalent approach, the technique used throughout much of this text is the risk-adjusted discount rate approach. This does not imply that the certainty equivalent approach is incorrect but rather that risk-adjusted discount rates tend to be more commonly used in real world practice.'

4. Running the risk

The 'risk-running' techniques to be discussed now are based on a simple intuitive idea. Instead of waiting for risk-laden events to unfold, we could make believe they do occur and observe the outcome. This 'What if' interrogation forms the general background of the two risk analysis techniques that follow: sensitivity analysis and Monte Carlo simulations.

4.1 Sensitivity analysis

In sensitivity analysis we try to see how operating results react when we change the variables involved. The process is simple: one or several variables are altered, calculations are reiterated and results are compared against those of other trials. Rather than adjusting to risk, we merely observe its effects by enacting most possible situations, from worst to best. Our attitude becomes empirical: What if mortgage rates shoot up to 18%? What if the vacancy rate drops 10%? What if leases go un-renewed for six months? What if ...?

Recent software developments have facilitated this kind of experimentation by providing built in 'What if' functions designed to check just how sensitive results are to variable fluctuations. The same technique also allows us to observe the relative importance of the input variables. Obviously, not all variables have the same effect on an investment's performance. For example, a sharp increase in water rates is practically inconsequential when compared to the major role played by mortgage rates. It is useful to measure the relative weight of each element included in the analysis and then calculate the elasticity (*i.e.*, the sensitivity) of results with regard to each variable. This can be accomplished either by reviewing results every time a variable is modified, or by making use of sensitivity functions in Excel.

An example, the Octavus Rozellus building, will serve to demonstrate the joys of sensitivity analysis. (By the way, you guessed right if you thought that this was the Rozy building's halfling.) (Table VII.3)

Table VIII.10   Introducing the Octavus Rosellus building.

Total Initial Purchase Price	100,000$
Mortgage Loan	80,000$
Nominal Rate	6%
Depreciation	15 years
Investor's Marginal Tax Rate	48.7%
Discount rate used in the NPV_c calculation (k_c)	10%
Disposition Price (10 times the NOI in year 6)	121,008$
Initial Potential Gross Income	15,000$
Gross Income Growth Rate	5%
Initial Operating Expenses	5,250$
Operating Expenses Growth Rate	3%
Vacancy Rate	5%

We could, for instance, analyse the impact of the capital structure (the debt to value ratio) upon the net present value of this property. In other words, we wish to determine how sensitive these results are to variations in the debt/value ratio.

The results are presented below in Table VIII.11.

Table VIII.11

D/V	Loan	NPV
0.9	90 000 $	13,971.06 $
0.8	**80 000 $**	**11,574.45 $**
0.7	70 000 $	9,177.84 $
0.6	60 000 $	6,781.23 $
0.5	50 000 $	4,384.62 $
0.4	40 000 $	1,988.01 $
0.3	30 000 $	-408.60 $
0.2	20 000 $	-2,805.21 $
0.1	10 000 $	-5,201.82 $

You may now indulge in another round of *'What if?'*, this time by toying with the equity discount rate (k_e) used in computing the net present value of equity. The results are displayed in Table VIII.12.

Table VIII.12

k_e	NPV_e
20%	771 $
19%	1,622 $
18%	2,516 $
17%	3,456 $
16%	4,444 $
15%	5,484 $
14%	6,578 $
13%	7,731 $
12%	8,945 $
11%	10,225 $
10%	**11,574 $**

These two examples were purposefully contrived to highlight a very common (and underestimated) danger of careless sensitivity analysis. The results should have convinced you of the NPV_E's great sensitivity to the capital structure and to the discount rate used in its calculation. The trouble is, the appropriate discount rate is a function of the capital structure: a highly leveraged investment should be discounted at a higher rate to make up for the extra risk. Since these variables are interdependent, you cannot reasonably change the debt to value ratio (D/V) without also changing the discount rate (k_e), a crime we wittingly committed in Table VIII.11 to illustrate how silly some sensitivity analysis can be (and often are...).

The problem is further complicated by the fact that the cost of debt (k_d) is also a function of D/V and in all likelihood, k_e is related to k_d. In fact, we must acknowledge that most important variables are mutually dependent for any given period. This issue is described as a problem of inter-variable dependency.

Furthermore, besides this inter-variable dependency, we also have to face up to inter-period dependency. In a dynamic model such as ours (in this case a five year holding period), we should expect a variable's level for one year to influence that of the following year and even temper that of other variables for the current year and those to come. For example, it is reasonable to assume that this year's rent level will largely dictate next year's rents (a case of intra-variable, inter-period dependency) and also affect next year's vacancy rate (a case of inter-variable and inter period dependency).

This inter-dependency lies at the very core of financial modelling and for this reason sensitivity analysis is very sensitive to inept handling. If you insist on using sensitivity analysis, you should tread cautiously and take these elementary precautions:

- when possible be explicit about the functional relationships linking variables (for example $k_e = k_a + (k_a - k_d) \times D/E$);
- use your best judgement when adjusting interdependent variables whose relationship cannot be formalized as above;
- keep the magnitude of variations minimal so as not to overlay disrupt inter-variable coherency: a 1% reduction of interest rates shouldn't perturb the structural nature of the problem, but a 10% change certainly will;
- basically, educated common sense should be applied generously to any and all sensitivity analysis.

These tips take on an even greater importance when it comes to our next risk-running technique: probabilistic simulations.

4.2 Monte Carlo simulation (probabilistic simulations)[1]

Probabilistic simulations are none other than the logical extension of sensitivity analysis. Instead of having the analyst choose the levels of a particular variable, a model repeatedly and randomly chooses points along the postulated probability distributions of any number of variables (these are dubbed 'control variables'). The calculation procedure appears in Figure VIII.10.

Figure VIII.10

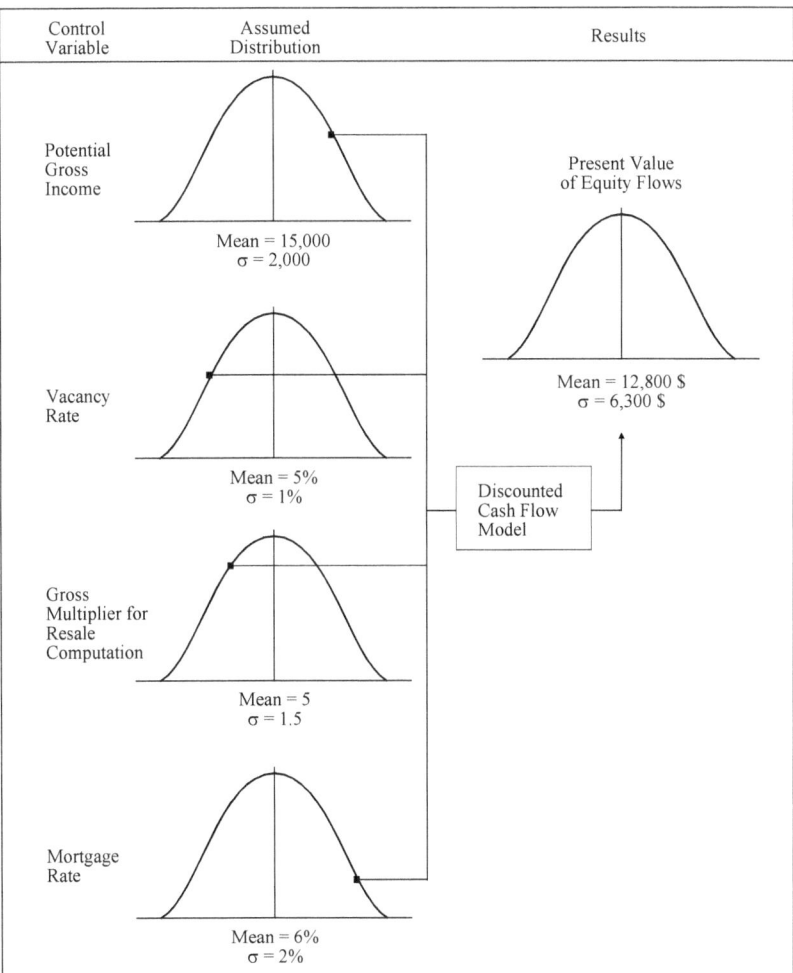

---

1. Monte Carlo stands for the analogy between the random selection along a probability distribution and the random selection of numbers in the game of Roulette at Monte Carlo, the Burswood of southern France.

A single point is randomly selected on each of the curves which best fits the expected behaviour of the control variables. The table below sums up the details of each of the control variables used in the Octavus Rozellus case:

Table VIII.13 Octavus Rosellus at Burswood (or Las Vegas ...)

Control variables	Normally Distributed with	
	Mean	Standard Deviation
Potential Gross Income	15 000 $	2 000 $
Vacancy Rate	5%	1%
Gross Income Multiplier for resale value	5	1.5
Mortgage rate	6%	2%

The Procedure is repeated 500 times, yielding 500 NPV_E values, which are then plotted as the net present value curve shown in Figure VIII.10. This curve roughly fits a normal distribution having a mean of 12,800$ and a standard deviation of about 6,300$. Using this distribution we could apply the traditional rules of statistical inference to 'bracket' our results and assign probabilities to various occurrences.

Simulation is too tempting an instrument not to be used recklessly. It also raises a host of practical and theoretical problems that cannot be fully covered here. The author does not put much faith in the results of its massive use in real estate analysis, but since simulation packages are now included in some advanced spreadsheet programs, most readers will have the opportunity to experiment with them and the following guidelines and warnings are in order:

- Do not perform simulations on the internal rate of return. We will expand on this in Appendix VIII.1, but be forewarned that some authors proceed obliviously and are surprised by the results;
- Try to use relatively independent control variables as we did in the previous example, otherwise you are liable to get tangled in the web of inter-variable dependency described in our discussion of sensitivity analysis. The problem becomes particularly acute here since *you* do not pick the values of the control variables: the random number generator does it for you;
- Use a risk-free discount rate (k_e = 4% was used here). Because you recreate a 'certain world' for each run, you do not want to double count the risk premium by randomizing your runs and discounting at a risk adjusted rate. This point is often overlooked and explains why results obtained by Monte Carlo analysis differ so markedly from those found by conducting a deterministic analysis on the same data;
- And, oh yes ... last piece of advice: do not do it by hand. It could tax your patience beyond repair.

5. Conclusion

We have now convinced ourselves of the ubiquity of investment risk and surveyed the ways and means of adjusting our valuation models in consequence. We can modify discount rates, convert cash flows into their certain equivalents or visualize the repercussions of risk through the use of sensitivity analyses and probabilistic simulations. Since most of these techniques suffer from various theoretical or empirical handicaps, choosing the right one boils down to practical considerations:

- Paper and pencil analysts will try to do their best to adjust discount rates in the general spirit of the Modigliani-Miller approach (see Appendix VI.1). They may even attempt to adapt certainty equivalent models, especially if good calculators are not at hand;

- Computer-equipped analysts will surely succumb to temptation and use sensitivity analyses: carried out with a good dose of circumspection, they do give valuable indications as to a project's probable performance;

- Those with access to advanced software may wish to try their hand at Monte Carlo analysis but they must remember that unbridled use of these simulations can only lead to obscure and costly results;

- Finally, we must concede that none of these techniques are commonly used in present real estate practice... a tardy but necessary admission. Decision-makers are generally too busy and unwilling to formulate problems in such formal terms. **The only viable prescription is to resort to scenario analysis**. A scenario is simply a diminutive of a full-scale sensitivity analysis where (for instance) only three coherent hypotheses are retained (optimistic - OK! - pessimistic), just as we did at the beginning of this chapter.

Excel-type spreadsheets offer very flexible access to scenario treatments and offer the almost costless way for the decision-maker to double check his projections and size up his results.

Appendix VI.1

Performance measurements: bells and whistles ...

1. Gross income criteria adjustments for valuers

The Gross Income Multiplier and its reciprocal, the rate of return on gross income, are also used as approximate but helpful instruments by valuers. When a given income property (the "subject" in the valuers' jargon) is reasonably similar to other properties which have been recently transacted on "the market," its value can be found as a multiple of the subject's gross income times the market GIM (the average GIM on recent market transactions):

$$V = GI \times GIM$$

If the operating characteristics of the subject property differ from the normal conditions (observed on "the market" for similar properties), an adjustment can be applied to the GIM valuation procedure. This adjusted GIM is obtained as follows:

a. the operating characteristics normally observed on the market are written $ß = NOI/GI$: the ratio of Net Operating Income to the Gross Income (the higher the expenses, the lower the ß ratio and conversely);

b. the operating characteristics of the subject property are written as $ß^* = NOI^*/GI^*$;

c. the adjusted GIM is then: GIM (adjusted) = GIM (market) × $ß^*/ß$

For example, assume that the market GIM is 6 for a normal operating structure represented by $ß = 0.60$ (*i.e.*, the expenses are 40% of the gross income and thus the net income is 60% of the gross income). Our Sextus subject property with an operating $ß^*$ of 0.75 will be appraised with an adjusted GIM of 7.5 (remember the expenses are 2,000$ out of a gross income of 8,000$):

GIM (adjusted) = 6 × (0.75/0.60) = 7.5

Thus the appraised value should be raised to 60,000$ (8,000$ × 7.5) since the Sextus' operating characteristics are much better than the ones normally found on the market (with a hypothetical ß ratio of 0.60).

2. From GIM to NIM

Let us also illustrate how to obtain the NIM directly from the GIM when we know the operating characteristics of a property (its ß).

We may write:

V = GI × GIM

And also:

V = GI/GRR

If we have the ratio of net income to gross income (NOI/GI = ß), we can link the gross and net concepts as shown below:

NOI = ß × GI

Then:

V = ß × GI/NRR

    = GI/GRR

Therefore:

NRR = ß × GRR

Or:

NRR = ß/GIM

And finally:

GIM = ß/NRR

For example with Sextus [GI = 8,000$, ß = 0.75% and GIM = 6], we derive the Value from the Gross Income:

V = 8,000$ × 6

   = 48,000$

And from the Net Operating Income:

NOI = 0.75 × 8,000$

     = 6,000$

And:

NRR = 0.75/6

     = 12.50%

Thus:

V = 6,000$/0.12

  = 48,000$

... *quod erat demonstrandum.*

3. The auto-financing price (PV*)

This variant form of the Net Income Multiplier is simply the maximum purchase price so that a property will pay its own way under 100% financing. In other words, it is the maximum property value (all debt) for which the Net Operating Income would exactly cover the debt payments.

If we write this auto-financing price (PV*) as the present value of a stream of NOI (which will be equal to the annual mortgage service) at the mortgage rate **i** (over **n** years) its value will be:

PV* = NOI × (P/A, i, n)

For Sextus, the Net Operating Income is 6,000$ or 500$ per month and the mortgage rate is i = 8% and thus PV* is 52,320$. If the purchaser pays this price, he will be able to meet a 100% debt repayment out of his Net Operating Income:

PV* = NOI (monthly) × (P/A, i, n)

   = 500$ × (P/A, i = 8%/12, 15 × 12)

PV* = 52,320$

If the purchaser does not borrow the full value of 52,320$, the return on his equity will then also be 8% (assuming no resale gain). But, since the investor should expect a higher return on his equity investment (he wants to make more than his banker), the auto-financing price should clearly be considered as a maximum price.

The relationship between this PV* and the Net Income Multiplier should now be quite obvious:

PV* = NOI × (P/A, i, n)

and:

NIM = $\frac{PV^*}{NOI}$ = (P/A, i, n)

Thus, the Net Income Multiplier is nothing more than the present value of a 1$ annuity (with annual compounding). This should suffice to explain why the NIM depends so directly on the prevailing mortgage market conditions: property values drop when mortgage rates go up and conversely. As a review exercise, the reader may wish to verify this important dual relationship between mortgage rates, operating ratios and value criteria (this is a neat little exercise to develop on your spreadsheet program).

4. Variants of the cash return measurements

Some professionals (and a few textbooks) advocate the use of a return measurement in which the principal amortisation of the mortgage loan (the equity buildup) is added to the before-tax cash flows.

In the following notation the DE stands for the increased equity accrued through the principal repayments. Equity builds up slowly during the first years of the amortisation but later repayment represents a larger share of the monthly payments. In light of this, the rate will be significantly higher than the previous one at the end of the amortisation period.

This new-look rate of return is written:

$$BT\Delta ER = \frac{\text{Before-Tax Cash Flow} + \text{Principal Amortisation}}{\text{Equity investment}}$$

or, equivalently:

$$BT\Delta ER = \frac{\text{Net Income} - \text{Interest Payments}}{\text{Equity investment}}$$

The objectionable aspect of this criterion is the fact that the annual equity buildup (DE) is not cash in your pocket. Its inclusion is not consistent with the all-cash nature of the other components of the return formula. Even if equity is being built up over the holding period (i.e., *if* no refinancing occurs and *if* the value of the property does not fall below the outstanding balance of the loan), this accumulated equity will not turn into effective cash until the property is sold and the mortgage fully reimbursed. Thus, at best, this equity buildup (DE) represents future cash, and as you certainly know by now, future dollars should never be mixed up with present dollars.

This state of affairs is certainly not improved by this souped-up version of the previous measurements:

$$BT\Delta ER = \frac{\text{Before-Tax Cash Flow} + \text{Average Amortisation}}{\text{Equity investment}}$$

where the average of 3 or 5 years equity buildup is included as a cash return. (By the way, why is this a souped-up version?)

And the lemon among the cash return measurements is probably this bastardised "static" criterion:

$$BT\Delta ER = \frac{\text{Before-Tax Cash Flow} + \Delta E \text{ over 3 years } + \Delta V \text{ over 3 years}}{\text{Equity investment}}$$

Here DE is the average equity buildup over 3 years and DV is the average appreciation of the property over 3 years.

In this last formula the heresies are piling up. Apples (cash) are added to oranges (equity buildup) in the numerator, then real equity increase (DE) is added to a hypothetical equity increase (DV) and, *abysus abysam invocat,* all the amounts are bunched up and averaged without any discounting.

None of the variants described above are acceptable. They flirt with pure hucksterism and they should not be used in a professional context.

5. From debt coverage ratio to security margin

The Security Margin Ratio is the complement of the Debt Coverage Ratio.

SMR = (NOI - PMT)/NOI

$$DCR = \frac{\text{Net Income - Debt Service}}{\text{Net Income}}$$

Let us clarify the complementary relationship between these two ratios by first rewriting the SMR in a more intuitive form:

PMT = NOI (1 - SMR)

Thus we have:

PMT/NOI = (1 - SMR)

And finally:

DCR = NOI/PMT = 1/(1 - SMR)

With Sextus, the respective rates and ratios are:

DCR = 6,000$/4,358 $
     = 1.37

SMR = (6,000$ - 4,358 $)/6,000$
     = 0.27

You may wish to verify that indeed the two ratios are equivalent:

DCR = 1/(1 - SMR)
1.37 = 1/(1 - 0.27)

Appendix VI.2

Return and financial leverage

The financial leverage concept derives its imagery from the fact that returns can be amplified by the proper use of debt in the same manner as the strength of an individual will be amplified by the proper positioning of a lever under a heavy load. This leverage effect is probably one of the most attractive characteristics of real estate investment since a down payment of 20% or less is normally sufficient to secure a property.

But the financial leverage effect, like the mythological Esope's tongue, can be the best and the worst of things: it can be favourable (boosting the equity returns) or unfavourable (with negative returns). In Australia the expression "financial gearing" may be used more commonly.

Whether it is glorified or vilified, the leverage effect can be described under different guises that will now be presented from the most naive (and fallacious) to the more refined (though not less fallacious) forms.

1. The naive leverage

Let us compare two real estate stories:

— A property is purchased for 100000$ cash and sold a year later for 150000$; the return on the investment is a mere 50%.

— The same property is financed on 80% of its value with a 10% interest only loan (the interest of 8000$ is paid at the end of the year). The return can be computed hereafter.

		Acquisition	Disposal
Equity		$E_0 = 20000\$$	$E_1 = 62000\$$
Debt	Outstanding	$D_0 = 80000\$$	$D_1 = 80000\$$
	Interest		$8000\$$
Value		$V_0 = 100000\$$	$V_1 = 150000\$$
BTER Before-Tax Return		$(E_1 - E_0)/E_0$ $(62000\$ - 20000\$)/20000\$ = 210\%$	

Of course the other side of the story could be slightly less exciting if we were now to assume that the disposal price is not 150000$ but simply 100000$

(equal to the purchase price). The non-levered investor will have a 0% rate of return, but the levered investor has now far less than he bargained for:

		Acquisition	Disposal
Equity		$E_0 = 20000\$$	$E_1 = 12000\$$
Debt	Outstanding	$D_0 = 80000\$$	$D_1 = 80000\$$
	Interest		$8000\$$
Value		$V_0 = 100000\$$	$V_1 = 100000\$$
BTER	$(E_1 - E_0)/E_0$		
Before-Tax Return	$(12000\$ - 20000\$)/20000\$ = -40\%$		

This very simple story exemplifies the very nature of the leverage effect: it amplifies the positive returns **and** the negative returns.

2. The naive leverage (slightly less ...)

We could now recycle the Sextus building to examine the effect of the financial structure on the equity returns. The following table expands on the results already presented in Table VI.6.

Table VI.2.1   The Sextus building: the leverage effect on annual returns

	1st case	2nd case	3rd case	4th case	5th case
Equity	5,000$	10,000$	15,000$	20,000$	48,000$
Debt	43,000$	38,000$	33,000$	28,000$	0
PMT ($k_d = 8\%$)	-4,028$	-3,560$	-3,091$	-2,623$	-
PMT ($k_d = 12.5\%$)	-5,674$	-5,014$	-4,354$	-3,694$	-
PMT ($k_d = 15\%$)	-6,652$	-5,879$	-5,105$	-4,332$	-
Value	48,000$	48,000$	48,000$	48,000$	48,000$
NOI	6,000$	6,000$	6,000$	6,000$	6,000$
Net Return on NOI	12.50%	12.50%	12.50%	12.50%	12.50%
BTER ($k_d = 8\%$)	39.44%	24.40%	19.39%	16.88%	12.50%
BTER ($k_d = 12.5\%$)	6.53%	9.86%	10.97%	11.53%	12.50%
BTER ($k_d = 15\%$)	-13.04%	1.21%	5.97%	8.34%	12.50%

Here again the favourable or unfavourable effects of the financing structure are illustrated. But, here we measure the effects in terms of annual operation returns whereas, previously, we illustrated the leverage effect in terms of disposal returns. The net rate of return of 12.5% (NRR = NOI/V) is, obviously, not influenced by the evolution of the debt-to-value ratio (D/V); but the equity return (BTER = (NOI - PMT)/E_0) increases along with D/V when the mortgage rate k_d is 10% and decreases along with the ratio D/V when the rate is 15%.

An intuitive conclusion could be derived from this illustration; the leverage is positive (favourable) when the mortgage rate is below the net rate of return and negative (unfavourable) when the debt is more expensive than the return on the property. This intuitive approach is fairly clear since you must remember that the net operating income is split between the owner and the debt holder. If the property return is below the cost of the debt, the debt holder receives a better return than the investor and the latter does not have an incentive to increase her debt load. Conversely if the rate of return on the property is greater than the cost of the debt; it seems to make sense to borrow more and thus to lever-up the cash returns.

Thus a simple rule is often suggested:

— If NRR > k_d, then the leverage is positive and the equity return will be greater than the net return: BTER > NRR;

— If NRR < k_d, then the leverage is negative and the equity return will be less than the net return: BTER < NRR.

3. The naive leverage (less and less naive …)

We could also combine the disposal leverage of the first kind with the operation leverage of the second kind; and, if we now include the taxation effects, we enter some choppy water and must use a dynamic indicator such as the Net Present Value and the Internal Rate of Return.

Many authors[1] and most textbooks[2] advocate a decision rule which is very similar to the previous rule but for the fact that the dynamic internal rate of return replaces the static cash and net returns.

The new rule is thus: the leverage is positive if the internal rate of return on the whole investment (noted k_a) is greater that the after-tax cost of debt. Since the interest on the mortgage is tax-deductible the after-tax cost of the debt is only k_d ¥ (1-TMT). [TMT is the marginal rate of taxation]. Thus a 15% mortgage costs only 9% if the marginal rate of taxation is 40% {15% (1 - 40%)}. When this condition is met, the equity return (k_e) will be greater than the total return (k_a) and the investor should increase her debt to value ratio.[3]

---

1. Zerbst and Cooley (1978), Lusht (1977).
2. Notably, in the otherwise excellent Jaffe and Sirmans' textbook op. cit. chapters 10 and 11.
3. This point may require a clarification. Let us compare two properties under different financing conditions: ($)

Net Operating income	100	100
Interest	- 50	0
Net taxable income	50	100
Income tax (50%)	- 25	- 50
Net after-tax income	25	50

    Thus the 50 $ interest is reduced to a 25 $ difference on the after-tax net income.

The complete rule is commonly stated as follows:

Favourable leverage $k_e > k_a$ when $k_a > k_d ¥ (1 - TMT)$
Unfavourable leverage $k_e < k_a$ when $k_a < k_d ¥ (1 - TMT)$
Neutral leverage $k_e = k_a$ when $k_a = k_d ¥ (1 - TMT)$

This very widely accepted and recommended rule is nevertheless incorrect and was justly denounced by J. Mao[1] who demonstrated that the simple "$k_e > k_a$ when $k_a > k_d ¥ (1 - TMT)$" rule may be inconsistent with the proper rule which should be expressed in terms of net present value. Unfortunately Mao's argument was marred by his inappropriate adjustment of the discount rate k_e used in the computation of the Net Present Value of the equity[2] and this brings us to the very famous Modigliani-Miller proposition 1.

4. No magic in leverage[3] in Liechtenstein

Franco Modigliani and Merton H. Miller[4] gained fame and at least one Nobel prize (Modigliani) for the startling discovery that the size of a pie is not increased when it is spliced in many shares. Or, in our context, they have demonstrated that the leverage effect has no influence on the value of the property. The division of the pie (the value) in two shares (the debt and the equity) does not increase the size of the pie — at least in Liechtenstein.[5]

A simple example will illustrate their very important point.

---

1. Mao, J., "*Wealth Maximizing Criterion for Profitable Leverage in Real Estate*", **The Real Estate Appraiser and Analyst**, 45, May-June 1979, p. 51-54.

2. Achour, D. and Hamilton, S., "*Financial Leverage in Real Estate Investments*", **ACFAS proceedings**, Montreal 1985 and also Achour, D., Seck, D. and Hamilton, S., "*Financial Mix and Investment Decision: the Effects of the Debt Parameter*", **ASAC proceedings**, Vancouver 1986.

3. The expression "*no magic in leverage*" is Stewart Myers' in "*The Capital Structure Puzzle*", **The Journal of Finance**, Vol. XXXIX, July 1984.

4. Modigliani, F. and Miller, M.H., "*The cost of capital, corporation finance and the theory of investment*", **American Economic Review**, June 1958, p. 261-297.

5. Liechtenstein is a country without income tax. The situation in the taxed world is more complex but the same results obtain according to Miller (M.R. Miller, "*Debt and Taxes*", **Journal of Finance**, p. 261-276, May 1977.). This position clearly contradicts most of the real life evidence (especially in the real estate industry) and has been convincingly questioned by many authors. Most notably Barnea, A., Haugen, R.A. and Senbet, L.W., "*Market imperfections, agency problems, and capital structure*", **Financial Management**, (Summer 1981); Harris et al., **Journal of Finance**, September 1983. The leverage puzzle is also approached in a innovative fashion by Myers (op. cit.) who introduces the "pecking order" concept.

Table VI.2.2 Leverage in Liechtenstein (in Swiss Francs)

Value of the property				100000 SF
Equity				20000 SF
Debt				80000 SF
Mortgage rate k_d (interest only)				10%
Hypothetical Net Operating income	5000 SF	8000 SF	10000 SF	15000 SF
Net Rate of Return (NRR or k_a1)	5%	8%	10%	15%
Debt Service	8000 SF	8000 SF	8000 SF	8000 SF
Cash Flows	-3000 SF	0	2000 SF	7000 SF
Equity Rate of Return (BTER or k_e)	-15%	0%	10%	35%

Here the financial leverage plays its usual amplifying trick of boosting the cash return from -15% to 35% when the net return goes from 5% to 15%. But, this increase in cash return **has no effect on the total value of the asset (nor on the investor's wealth) since the discount rate should be adjusted to take into account the increased financing risk implied by the increased debt to value ratio**. For example, with a Net Operating Income of 10000 SF, the total value of the property can be written as the value of a perpetual flow of net income discounted at the k_a:

V_A = NOI/k_a
    = 10000 SF/10%
    = 100000 SF

Whereas the value of the equity (with a 80% D/V ratio) is now:

V_E = $BTCF/k_e$
    = 2000 SF/10%
    = 20000 SF

If we put together the two shares of the pie, we will find its full value:

V_A = Debt + Equity
    = 80000 SF + 20000 SF
    = 100000 SF

Now let us perform the same demonstration for a NOI of 15 000 SF:

V_A = NOI/k_a
    = 15000 SF/15%
    = 100000 SF
V_E = $BTCF/k_e$
    = 7000 SF/35%
    = 20000 SF

---

1. Net return = k_a and cash return = k_e. If the property is held indefinitely, static indicators will be equivalent to dynamic indicators.

V_A = Debt + Equity
    = 80000 SF + 20000 SF
V_A = 100000 SF

Q.E.D. and not trivial at all...

What has to be clearly understood is that the discount rate must be adjusted to take into account the increasing financial risk borne by the investor when the ratio D/V (or also E/V and D/E) are increased. The riskier the investment the higher should be the expected cash returns. We generally accept the idea that the risk-taking investor must be rewarded with a higher return, but beyond this intuitive truism the functional relationship can be clarified.

The value of an unlevered perpetual asset is written:

V_A = NOI/k_0 (N.B.: $k_0 = k_a$, when D/V = 0)

When leverage is introduced, the asset's rate of return is a combination of the cost of the debt (k_d) and the expected return on the equity investment (k_e). These two rates, weighted by the respective share of debt and equity, can be combined as an average rate (also called the weighted average cost of capital):

k_a = k_d x D/V + k_e ¥ E/V
       the debt factor   the equity factor

With the help of some algebra we derive k_e:

k_e = k_a + (k_a - k_d) ¥ D/E

This fundamental linear relationship is illustrated in Figure VI.2.1. Later on we will make use of this formula to adjust the discount rate of the equity model.

Figure VI.2.1

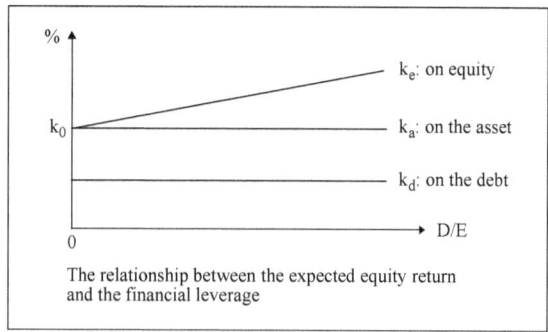

The relationship between the expected equity return and the financial leverage

Appendix VI.3

The Napkin and Yoyo techniques

The operating and financing ratios described in Chapter VI can be combined to build simple but useful decision tools which, despite their apparent rusticity, are used quite commonly by serious professional investors.

1. The «Napkin» technique[1]

With this technique the likely investment value of a property can be found on the sole basis of the net operating income and the financing conditions. Rozy will again serve as our guinea pig.

Table VI.3.1 Required information for a 'Napkin' treatment of Rozy

First year net operating income	NOI	15 000 $
Before-tax expected equity return	k^*_e	18%
Mortgage rate ($i_{1,1}$)	k_d	15%
Amortisation	n	25 years
Debt coverage ratio	DCR	1.20

Figure VI.3.1

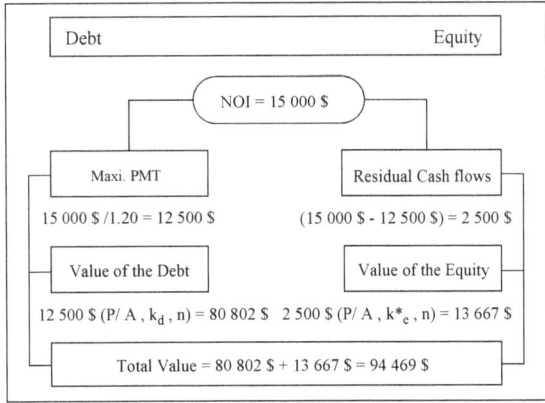

---

1. The usual denomination of this technique is the 'back of the envelope technique' (G. Gau et al. op. cit. p. 9-7). My Canadian students decided that they needed more space and opted for the paper napkins laid on the restaurant tables. So it goes!

The property brings in 15000$ for the first year. The investor expects a 18% equity return (before-tax) and knows that she will be able to secure a loan with a debt coverage ratio of 1.20. Under the prevailing market conditions (k_d = 15% on 25 years) such a ratio would allow a 12500$ annual mortgage payment (PMT maximum = NOI/1.20) which could amortise a total debt of 80802$ [Debt = PMT ¥ (P/A , k_d , n)].

Out of the 15000$, 2500$ is left in the investor's pocket (BTCF = NOI - PMT; 2500$ = 15000$ - 12500$) and this residual cash, treated as a perpetuity, is worth 13667$ [2500 ¥ (P/A , k^*_e , n)].

The investor would thus be willing to bid 94469$ for this property, 13667$ in the form of equity and a loan of 80802$.[1]

2. The Yoyo technique

Here we step into the promoter's shoes. If we know the production cost of a building, we can find the minimal rental rate required to realize a profitable investment. Conversely, if we know the prevailing rental conditions on a specific market we may determine the maximum building cost that we could accept for a given project.

On the downside (Figure VI.3.2), if we initially know the construction cost and the land cost per square meter, the physical parameters (number of storeys, total area, general design, constraints, etc.) we can derive the total construction cost and thus the required annual Net Operating Income to justify such a cost [V = NOI/(A/P, i , n)]. If we also have the ratio of effective rental use (the ratio of leasable area to total area) and the operating ratio (Net Operating Income/Gross Income), we can find the required gross rental rate.

On the upside, if we know the prevailing rental rates for this specific type of building we could step up to the total construction cost and judge the project's feasibility.

Thus, as with a Yoyo, you run the numbers from top to bottom and from bottom to top to 'iterate' a reasonable set of assumptions on the constructions costs, the physical characteristics of the product and the diverse rental condi-

---

1. This technique is very similar to the band of investment method suggested to calculate a cap. rate (See Fischer's 'Property Valuation Methodology'. Here the overall rate would be:

   R = D/V × f + E/V × k^*_e

      = (80802$/94469$) × 0.1546 + (13667$/94469$ × 0.1829

      = 15.87%

   And thus we obtain the value:

   V = 15000$/0.1587

     = 94469$

tions. This rudimentary sensitivity analysis (see Chapter VIII) is intuitively gratifying, cheap and can also be performed on a napkin.

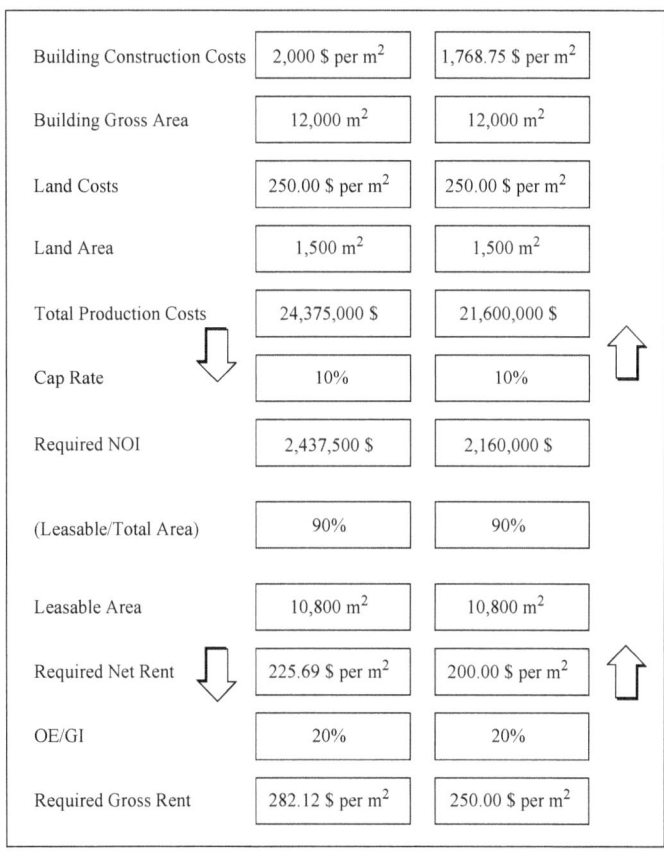

Figure VI.3.2: Analysing up and down, like a Yoyo

Appendix VII.1

The negative about negative gearing

Like most taxation traps "negative gearing schemes" are good ideas turned into confusion.

The concept is fairly simple. Since interest are deductible from taxable incomes, a property[1] may generate negative income taxes (a tax loss) that can be used to reduce other incomes.

So far, so good ... but three basic points must be kept in mind.

The loss must be temporary

The idea behind this tax provision is simply that many investments cannot be profitable immediately and that it may take one or more years to reach some positive return. But, ultimately, the investment must become profitable. The ATO position is quite clear about this point: a tax loss is allowable when there is a reasonable expectation of profit. If an investment is structured only to "loose money", the interest deduction may be disallowed (Tax ruling 95/33).

A loss is a loss ...

A negatively geared property loses some "fake" money (depreciation and building allowance) but mostly it loses "real" money in the form of operating expenditures and mortgage payments. These cash shortfalls have to be covered with after-tax dollars from other sources until the investment becomes profitable or until the property is sold, hopefully at a profit.

You need a gain at the end of the game

This profit at disposal should, after tax, be sufficient to cover the capitalised value of previous shortfalls. In other words the expected capital gains should cover all the losses, the taxes and the various headaches...

A successful negatively geared (negatively levered) investment is thus based on a triple gamble:

— the tax losses must be considered fully allowable deduction by the ATO;

— other incomes must be sufficient to offset the property cash losses;

---

1. And any other type of similar levered investment.

— the eventual capital growth must be high enough to insure that the net value of the investment is positive at a discount rate which is rewarding enough to cover the gambling risk and to compare with alternative investments.

The reader is invited to check[1] what are the conditions that would be required to successfully gear the Rozy property. In the following slightly modified version of Rozy, the resale value should be based on a multiplier of, at least, 15.8 times the net income (a cap. rate of 6.3%) to obtain a net present value equal to zero and thus to justify the negative gearing strategy. This is certainly a high gamble...

In this table, only the elements in bold were modified from the original Rozy all the other hypothesis are maintained. Thus we can observe that it does not take too much of a bad patch of luck to get into trouble.

Table VII.1.1   Schnegative gearing ... on Rozy

Acquisition value	$100,000
Disposal	
Net income multiplier	**15.82**
Disposal price	**$116,807**
Selling expenses (% of gross selling price)	4%
After-tax expected rate of return	**15%**
Years of operation (max of 10 years)	5
Initial Potential Gross Income	$15,000
Growth rate for the PGI	**2%**
Vacancy rate	**15%**
Initial operation expenses	$5,250
Rate of growth of operation expenses	**5%**
Marginal tax rate	48%

---

1. The Excel treatment of this type of problem requires the use of the Goal functions.

Appendix VIII.1

A Further drawback of the Internal Rate of Return

In studying the Octavus Rosellus project, we might have been inclined to apply the same probabilistic treatment to the Internal Rate of Return. Unfortunately, the IRR does not allow linear transformations nor does it tolerate probabilistic manipulations.

Let's use an example to illustrate this point (Table VIII.1.1).

Two projects (or market conditions) A and B have associated probabilities of p_A and p_B (with p_A and $p_B = 50\%$).

Table VIII.1.1 Of the additivity of NPV and IRR (in sesterces)

	Outlay	$ATCF_t$				NPV at a 10% discount rate	IRR
Years		1	2	3	4		
Project A	-1 000	-100	-150	-300	2 100	-74.24	8.24%
Project B	-1 000	200	400	500	900	502.76	26.80%
Project A + B	-1 000	50	125	100	1 450	214.26	16.02%

Now let's demonstrate how the NPV can be linearly transformed while the IRR can't.

$E(NPV)$ = $E(NPV_A + NPV_B)$ = $p_A (NPV_A) + p_B (NPV_B)$
= 214.26 sesterces = 0.5 (-74.24) + 0.5 (502.76)

Whereas: $E(IRR_A + IRR_B)$ = 16.03%

But: $p_A(IRR_A) + p_B(IRR_B)$ = 17.52%

For this reason, you should refrain from performing probabilistic manipulations on the IRR, especially in Monte Carlo type simulations.

www.ingramcontent.com/pod-product-compliance
Lightning Source LLC
Chambersburg PA
CBHW070240230526
45470CB00002B/464